Pan Breakthrough Books

Pan Breakthrough Books open the door to successful self-education. The series provides essential knowledge using the most modern self-study techniques.

Expert authors have produced clear explanatory texts on business subjects to meet the particular needs of people at work and of those studying for relevant examinations.

A highly effective learning pattern, enabling readers to measure progress step-by-step, has been devised for Breakthrough Books by the National Extension College, Britain's leading specialists in home study.

Michael Herbert lectures at South Devon Technical College, having taught previously at Somerset College of Arts and Technology. He has been a moderator at National level for the Business Education Council since 1979 and is Chief Examiner for the Associated Examining Board's O (Alternative) level paper in Business Studies.

Pan Breakthrough Books

Other books in the series

Pan Breakthrough Books

Practical Accounts 1

Michael Herbert

A Pan Original
Pan Books London and Sydney

Acknowledgement

I would like to thank John Meed of the National Extensions College for his advice, and my wife Jane for her encouragement, helpful suggestions and hard work in producing the typescript.

First published 1983 by Pan Books Ltd,
Cavaye Place, London SW10 9PG

© Michael Herbert 1983

ISBN 0 330 28057 0

Photoset by Parker Typesetting Service, Leicester
Printed in Great Britain by
Richard Clay (The Chaucer Press) Ltd,
Bungay, Suffolk

If you wish to study the subject matter of this book in more depth, write to the National Extension College, 18 Brooklands Avenue, Cambridge CB2 2HN, for a free copy of the Breakthrough Business Courses leaflet. This gives details of the extra exercises and professional postal tuition which are available.

Contents

Introduction

Practical Accounts I is an introduction to book-keeping and accounting which will be of immediate benefit to trainee ledger clerks, self-employed businessmen and examination students alike. Having read this book and completed all its suggested tasks you should be able to tackle with confidence the recording of transactions, preparation of statements and balancing of accounts, whether in a practical or classroom situation.

While writing this book I have tried to keep in mind a clear picture of you, the reader. I have tried to foresee the difficulties you will encounter as you grapple for the first time with ledger accounts, as you get to know the balance sheet, and as you finally master the joys of double entry book-keeping. Unlike the many students I have taught in the classroom you will be unable to ask questions of me but I hope I have anticipated where your queries will be and I have done my best to answer all your possible problems as they might occur.

As with all Pan Breakthrough texts this book is intended as a self-study, self-assessment text. Whether you intend to study the subject for an examination course or simply to enable you to keep your own books in better order, this book should be of assistance to you. If you have enrolled for a class or correspondence course then you will receive extra support. However, if you use this book as intended, you should be able to master the subject for yourself.

1 | The need for accounts

Most people associate accounting with the world of business. To see what it involves we can divide it into three parts.

First, it concerns the recording of transactions. This aspect is known as book-keeping because, at one time, most records or accounts were kept in books. Second, it involves reporting to people wanting information about the state of the business. This is called financial accounting because such reporting provides information in monetary or financial terms. Third, it is associated with controlling what is happening within a business. This is generally known as management accounting because managers are the people responsible for making the decisions which control what goes on.

There is nothing so special about accounting that it must be done only by accountants. We all do it, or could do it. Take for example John, a sixth-form student who works in a shop each Saturday. Most of his earnings used to disappear fairly quickly on clothes, records and concerts. Recently, however, John started to save. He wanted a motorbike. His parents agreed to buy him one for his next birthday, which was six months away, provided that by that time he could show them that he would be able to pay all the usual expenses involved in running a bike.

To help John do this, his mum gave him a pocket book. He wrote down his earnings each week and kept a note of his spending. When his birthday came he was able to show his parents exactly how much he had saved and how he had done it. By then he had also looked into the costs of running a motorbike including fuel, road tax, insurance and repairs. Writing down his savings for the previous six months on one side of a sheet of paper and the estimated running costs on the other, he was able to prove to his parents that he would indeed be able to run the bike – just.

John got his bike. He didn't throw away his pocket book, though. He soon found how useful it was in helping to keep a check on what it cost him to run the bike. He was often having to decide things like whether he should use the bike every day to travel to school (his bus pass was free); when to have the bent mud-guard repaired; who would service the bike most thoroughly and yet not charge too much; and how much he could put towards the crash helmet his girlfriend needed. He was able to use the information in his pocket book to help him make these decisions.

Self-check

When did John act as **a** book-keeper; **b** financial accountant; **c** management accountant?

ANSWER

He acted as **a** when keeping a record of his earnings, etc. in his pocket book. Recording transactions is what book-keeping is all about.

He acted as **b** when proving to his parents on a sheet of paper that he could afford to run the bike. Reporting to interested parties is the function of a financial accountant.

He acted as **c** when using the information in his pocket book to decide things like when he could afford to have his mud-guard repaired. Using accounts as an aid to decision making is the work of a management accountant.

If you had any difficulty with this question, reread the definitions on page 7.

So even if you do not use what you learn from this book in a business situation you may find it useful in your personal life. See if you can prove this yourself by attempting the following.

Activity

Make a list of ways in which you could (or already do) benefit from using basic accounting techniques.

RESPONSE

There are many benefits you might mention. On the book-keeping side it is always helpful to keep records of receipts and payments made through a bank account. When you receive your statement it is then much easier to check it. A record of spending on particular items might also be useful, e.g. heating, motoring or purchases of food for the freezer. It is sometimes helpful to prepare a clear statement of your financial position. Such a statement may help to persuade a bank manager to give you a loan or it might help to prove to yourself or others how much better off you are after giving up smoking. So drawing up a report rather like a financial accountant is useful. Everybody has to make decisions and very often these involve money. A housewife who is finding it difficult to make ends meet might be faced with the task of deciding whether her children should have school lunches or take their own. Another might have to decide whether they can afford a holiday this year and, if so, what sort. Simple records and brief statements will be very useful in making such decisions. No matter that they are written on the back of an envelope! Perhaps management accounting seems too grand a title for it. What's in a name? The word 'economics' derives from a Greek word meaning management of a household. House-wives are managers, so why shouldn't they use the techniques of management accounting?

Let's turn now to the business world. There are many different sorts of businesses. One way of classifying them is according to how they are owned. Among the most numerous are sole traders, who are also known as sole proprietors or sole owners. Here one person owns the business. Other types include part-nerships, limited companies, cooperatives and public corpora-tions. As far as accounting is concerned these are beyond the scope of this book, in which it is intended to consider only the type of business owned by one person.

A typical example of such an organisation is the building and decorating business owned by Henry Plunkett. Besides general repairs and decorating he also does quite a number of extensions. He employs six people. Try to acquaint yourself with the administration of this sort of business by attempting the following.

Activity

Make a list of different sorts of information that such a business will need to record.

RESPONSE

I would expect him to keep records or accounts of purchases of materials, payments made to suppliers of materials and services, invoices sent to customers, money received from customers, possessions of the business such as cash, premises, equipment and vehicles, money owed to creditors, e.g. the bank, wages paid to employees, income tax and national insurance deducted from employees' wages and value added tax paid on purchases or charged to customers.

Your list may be longer than mine but even if it only contains a few items it is still clear that records will need to be kept. Therefore book-keeping is essential.

Financial accounting is also of vital importance to Henry's firm. He will need to know how successful he is. This can be shown best by preparing a profit and loss account, which measures the amount of profit or loss made in a particular period of time, usually a year. Henry is not the only one who will be interested in what it reveals. The Inspector of Taxes (Inland Revenue) will want to know. People who own businesses do not pay tax weekly or monthly as do employees under the 'pay-as-you-earn' scheme. Their tax is assessed according to the amount of profit earned each year.

Henry would also like to know how much his business is worth. One way of showing this is by preparing a balance sheet. This shows the financial position of the business at a particular moment of time. In this respect it differs from the profit and loss account which covers a period of time.

Self-check

Ginger Jenkins has started a business similar to that of Henry. He does not keep proper records but reckons that, as long as he has plenty of cash coming in, he must be doing all right and therefore has no need of financial accounts or accountants. Who will dispute Ginger's freedom to run his business this way?

ANSWER

His Inspector of Taxes, who will require evidence on which to base his assessment of how much tax he should pay. When people do not provide enough satisfactory evidence the inspector has power to estimate how much profits have been made and tax them accordingly. It is usual in such circumstances to make such an estimate err on the high side rather than the low. This usually brings characters like Ginger to their senses. Of course, Ginger does not have to employ an accountant to prepare a profit and loss account and balance sheet. He could do it himself. If he reads this book he might be able to do so.

To be successful, Henry Plunkett will also find management accounting a great help as decision making is important in all businesses. Some people have a knack for making the right decisions, relying mainly on intuition. Others frequently choose incorrectly. However lucky a businessman may be, decisions made with knowledge of all relevant facts, including financial information, have most chance of being right in the long run.

The decisions Henry will have to make will be many and varied. Consider just one. Henry has been invited to submit an estimate to convert a farmer's barn into a home for his son and daughter-in-law. How will Henry go about this task? To begin he will need to know what the end product is to be like and what materials are to be used in its construction. An architect's drawing will provide much of the information he needs.

Given this, he will be able to calculate the amount of materials needed and the number of hours he thinks it will take to complete. He can then work out the cost of these materials and the amount of wages he will have to pay his men while they are working on this job. Information on the cost of materials will come from catalogues and recent invoices received for similar materials. For the wages cost he will be able to consult records of the various wage rates paid to his men, some of whom will be skilled and others unskilled. He will, of course, want to earn a profit for himself in return for taking on the risk involved in carrying out the job. Other considerations that might affect the final total figure he gives for the job include how badly he needs the work and whether it is likely that other firms will be able to give an estimate below his. Henry's experience will be invaluable in drafting the estimate for the farmer. Without the facts provided by his accounting records, however, it is clear that the preparation of the estimate would be much more of a hit-or-miss affair.

Activity

Think of some other decisions that Henry might have to make in managing his business. Consider if accounting would help him in making them.

RESPONSE

Decisions you could mention include: should he take on extra staff when trade is booming or rely on subcontracting some of the work to other firms? Should he purchase or lease the new equipment needed? If he decides to purchase, what is the best way of paying for it? Should he expand with money that will have to be borrowed? What is the best way of persuading his customers to pay him more promptly? Which is better, buying materials for cash to obtain lower prices or on credit to give him time to pay? Of course there are many more, but whatever management decision you thought of it is inevitable that it would best be made by reference to book-keeping records and the financial accounts. In larger businesses management accountants would probably draft individual statements to assist in making each such decision. In smaller businesses this is less likely.

Having seen the use of accounting to all of us as individuals and to business owners like Henry, it should not be too difficult for you to look further afield for other examples of its use. For instance many businesses are much larger than Henry's and are involved in different activities. Many employees in such businesses will be working with accounts and not all of them will be in the financial department. They may well be employed in marketing, production or personnel departments.

There are other forms of business ownership. Partnerships need accounts to satisfy each partner that the profits are being fairly divided and companies are accountable to their shareholders. Local and central government provide a variety of services and will need accounts, not least for keeping a check on the money they receive from ratepayers and taxpayers.

Review

1 Complete the following sentences:

   a Recording transactions is known as _____ because at one time most accounts were kept in _____.

   b Reporting on the state of a business by means of statements such as _____ and _____ accounts and balance sheets is known as _____ _____.

   c Using accounts as an aid in controlling and managing a business is known as _____ _____.

   d The above activities together make up the subject matter of _____.

2 What sort of business, from the point of view of ownership, is that of Henry Plunkett?

3 Give three examples of information that a business like Henry's would need to record. In each case say why this information should be recorded.

4 Which of the following is unlikely to be involved in any way with accounting: business owner, salesman, wages clerk, personnel manager, marketing director, inspector of taxes, treasurer of a tennis club, housewife?

ANSWERS

1 The missing words in order are: **a** book-keeping, books; **b** profit, loss, financial accounting; **c** management accounting; **d** accounting.

If this caused any difficulty reread the definitions on pages 7 and 10.

2 Henry is a sole proprietor or sole trader because he alone owns the business.

3 The three examples that come most readily to my mind are:

   a Money received and paid. Money is the lifeblood of all businesses and a close check must be kept on it.

   b Amounts owing to suppliers. Credit is important to many businesses, none of which want to lose this facility. Care must be taken not to offend suppliers by being too slow in payment.

   c Amounts due from customers. Many customers have to be asked more than once for the money they owe.

   There are other examples on page 10 to which you can refer if necessary. A reason should occur to you for each one. Besides individual reasons you might also have given general ones. For example all such information is needed for an owner to know how successful he is. It will be needed to calculate profits and losses. Such information is also needed to satisfy the Inspector of Taxes. It is also useful in providing the material needed to aid decision making.

4 Your general knowledge together with what you have read in this chapter should have led you to say 'None'. If you have any doubts about this find out what each of them does and reconsider.

2 | Starting a business

Finding the right business

When Bill Turner was made redundant he decided that he would never again work for someone else. He wanted to be his own boss! After thinking over a number of ideas he decided that he would like to purchase a shop. The sort of shop he had in mind was a general store which sold a variety of things but which concentrated on food and groceries. He reasoned that these were items which everybody needed and would give his business a reasonable amount of safety. Bill's wife, Joan, had been complaining for several years about the dirtiness of the town in which they lived – buying a shop in a Devon village seemed a good way of satisfying both his wife's and his own ambitions.

Selling their semi-detached house realised £12,000 after the mortgage had been repaid to their building society. This, together with Bill's redundancy payment of £10,000, meant that they had a total of £22,000 of their own money to invest in a business.

Many people would have spent a great deal of time talking to shopkeepers, bank managers and business agents before making a decision to spend their £22,000. Not Bill! He had always been quick at making decisions and this time proved to be no exception. He spent one weekend in Devon, looked at five properties and agreed to buy one of them for £30,000. Only then did he approach his bank manager and ask for a loan of £8,000 to meet the difference between the buying price and their available capital.

After listening to Bill rave about the potential of the business, the bank manager looked carefully at a copy of the accounts and agreed to advance the loan. This was made subject to a favourable report from a representative of the bank, which would be completed after visiting the premises.

Self-check

Suppose a mistake had been discovered in the calculation of Bill's redundancy payment and that he was only entitled to £7,000. What is the most they would have been able to pay for a business?

ANSWER

If you have calculated that the maximum price they could pay was £27,000 you are correct. The answer could be calculated in this way:

	£
Net amount realised from house sale	12,000
add Redundancy payment	7,000
add Loan from the bank	8,000
Total finance available to purchase a business	27,000

Alternatively you would have said that the mistake reduced their available finance by £3,000 (original redundancy payment calculation of £10,000 less the corrected calculation of £7,000). This would therefore reduce the amount they could afford to pay for a business by £3,000. Hence:

	£
Previous possible finance	30,000
less Reduction in redundancy payment	3,000
New possible finance	27,000

Of course this assumes that only the redundancy payment changed. It is possible that one or more of the other sources of finance could also vary. For instance, they could attempt to persuade the purchasers of their house to pay more for it. They might be able to persuade their bank manager to give them a bigger loan or they might be able to obtain a further loan elsewhere. Any one of these (or a combination of them) might be enough to offset the reduced redundancy payment. If none were possible all might still not be lost. The sellers of the shop might take a price reduction.

It must be realised that all the factors we have mentioned might vary. Indeed in many business deals negotiation and haggling continue up to the last moment. In the end, it is essential for the finance available to be enough to pay for the business being bought. In other words if Bill and Joan have to pay a purchase price of £30,000 (including expenses of legal fees, etc.) they must find this sum either from their own resources or from other people. Most probably they will rely on a combination of both. Luckily for Bill and Joan no mistake had been made in calculating Bill's redundancy payment and the deal was able to go through exactly as described.

We are going to use Bill's shop (as well as other sorts of business) to learn about a number of the basic principles of accounting. One has been established already:

● *The sources of finance available must equal the purchase price of a business.*

The balance sheet
In this chapter we take a preliminary look at a question which is of great importance to the owner, or possible future owner, of a firm: how much is the business worth? This will lead us to analyse a business statement of which you may well have heard – the balance sheet. If you haven't, don't worry because I will start with the assumption that you know nothing whatsoever about business accounts. When you understand what a balance sheet is and what it contains, you should be able to draft a balance sheet from information provided.

The business which Bill purchased had been run unsuccessfully for several years. Because of this he had been able to buy it for an amount which just equalled the value of the premises, fixtures and fittings and stock-in-trade. These are called the assets of a business. Assets are basically the possessions of the business on which a money value can be placed. If the business had been more successful the sellers might have been able to demand a price higher than the value of the assets purchased. This would have been to buy something called the goodwill of the business. Goodwill is the benefit obtained from buying a business which has good connections and a good reputation. As the previous owner had not been successful, little or no goodwill existed. Hence Bill was able to buy the business for the agreed value of the assets.

When a new business starts it is a good idea to draw up a statement showing its financial position. One way of doing this is in the form of a balance sheet. Look carefully at the following statement.

Balance sheet of Valuemart as at 1 July 1976

Sources of finance	£	Assets	£
Proprietor's capital	22,000	Premises	26,000
		Fixtures and fittings	2,000
Liabilities		Stock	2,000
Bank loan	10,000	Cash at bank	1,900
		Cash in hand	100
	32,000		32,000

From this we can derive a definition of a balance sheet. It is a statement drawn up at a particular date (in this case 1 July 1976) to show the value of the assets of the business (which Bill had decided to call Valuemart) and how the finance for these assets was obtained.

Self-check

Define 'assets' and give some examples of the sort of things that might be included as 'fixtures and fittings' in the above shop.

ANSWER

'Assets' are those possessions or advantages a business has on which a money value can be placed. There are, of course, some advantages on which it is not possible to place a definite money value; for instance the effort that Bill expects to put into the business or the hard work he expects from Joan.

Examples of items which might count as 'fixtures and fittings' in a general store are: shelving, counters, displays, fridge and the till.

The sources of finance may be divided into two types: first the finance provided by the owner, which is called the proprietor's capital or sometimes simply the capital. In this case the proprietor is Bill Turner himself. His wife Joan was prepared to help him but did not want to be considered as an owner of the business. The second source of finance is called liabilities. This is the money owing to people outside the business which has been used to finance some of the assets of the business. In this case the only liability is to the bank which agreed to lend Bill some of the money he needed to buy the business. People, or other organisations like the bank, to whom money is owed are called the creditors of the business.

Self-check

Have you noticed anything unusual about the amount of the bank loan? How would you account for this?

ANSWER

You may have remembered that Bill needed a loan of only £8,000 to top up his own capital of £22,000 by enough to buy the business for £30,000 (see page 15). The loan in the balance sheet is £2,000 greater than he originally requested. If you look carefully at the balance sheet you will see that there are two assets which together are worth £2,000 and which were not actually purchased by Bill. These are cash in hand and cash at bank. All businesses need both very ready money (cash in hand) and money which can be obtained fairly quickly (cash in the bank). It is likely that Bill will have realised that and returned to his bank manager with a request for a further loan. It is also possible that the bank manager himself will have suggested Bill should have the extra finance which should be kept readily available. In any case it is clearly necessary for a business to have some money for use when needed. For example more stock may be required from the local cash-and-carry or a broken window might have to be repaired.

The balance sheet on page 18 is only one way of presenting the information contained in it – later on you will discover other ways of doing it. One virtue of the way in which it is shown in this chapter is that it makes very clear the relationship between sources of finance and assets. In any business the value of capital and liabilities which make up the sources of finance equals the value of the assets. This is known as the book-keeping equation and we can use it to reduce Bill Turner's opening balance sheet to the simple form of:

capital (£22,000) + *liabilities* (£10,000) = *assets* £32,000.

If we know the value of two items in this equation it is always possible to calculate the third. The equation can be turned around to read:

capital = assets less *liabilities*

or *liabilities = capital* less *assets*.

Self-check

To make sure you understand this, complete the table below by filling in the missing figure for each of the four separate businesses.

Business	Capital £	Liabilities £	Assets £
a	10,000	5,000	
b		16,000	30,000
c	12,000		37,000
d		60,000	50,000

ANSWER

Your calculations should have revealed the following missing figures: **a** assets £15,000, **b** capital £14,000, **c** liabilities £25,000, **d** capital − £10,000.

The first three calculations should have presented no problems. If you had difficulty reread the section about the book-keeping equation. The fourth calculation perhaps required a little more thought. What has happened here is that the business concerned has been so unsuccessful that its assets are not sufficient to pay off all the liabilities. Thus if the assets were sold for

£50,000 some of the creditors of the business would not receive the money that was due to them. £10,000 would be left unpaid and the owner of the business would be responsible for meeting these extra debts himself. The 'negative capital' is called a deficiency of capital.

If you are not happy working with negative figures you could rewrite the book-keeping equation to read:

liabilities = assets + deficiency.

But remember, this only applies when the liabilities are greater than the assets.

A firm which has liabilities greater than its assets is said to be insolvent. Naturally this sort of position would not be allowed to continue for very long. Once the creditors knew about it they would be afraid things would become worse and that they might lose even more of what was owed to them. The bankruptcy court is only a small step away for a businessman who finds himself in such a difficult financial position.

We will now return to the question posed earlier in the chapter: how much is that business worth?

A straightforward answer, and a perfectly acceptable one, is that anything, including a business, is worth what you can persuade someone to pay for it. Bill had made his decision on which business to buy very quickly and you must not think that all purchasers are alike in this respect. While he was prepared to pay £30,000 for it, he did not have all the finance he needed and he had to rely on his bank manager for a loan to complete the deal. The bank manager looked carefully at the accounts before making his decision. Among these accounts would have been the last balance sheet of the business being sold.

The bank manager would want to make certain that a loan to Bill would be secure. He would want the value of the assets of the business to be more than enough to cover the amount of the loan. In fact he would probably have insisted that, in the event of failure, the bank should have first claim on the assets of the business. This would enable the bank to recover its money. It could be done by means of a mortgage on the property. In a similar way a house buyer takes out a mortgage with a building society in order to have enough money to buy his house.

The bank manager would also have been looking after Bill's interests. If he thought that the business was not a good buy he would not be regarded as a competent financial adviser if he did not point that out. Safety of the loan is only one consideration. His client's satisfaction is another. Both the bank and Bill will be happy if the business is successful: Bill, for the obvious reason that it is his business and the profits belong to the owner; the bank, for the reason that if the business is successful, Bill will have no difficulty paying the interest charged on the loan. The bank will thus make a profit as well as helping one of its clients to do the same. Trying to make sure that the business was indeed worth what Bill was prepared to pay for it was therefore important to his bank manager.

Exercise

The balance sheet below relates to one of the businesses Bill looked at but did not buy. From the information contained in it, say how much you think it is worth to its owner. If you have to assume anything in order to do this, make a note of it.

Balance sheet of Rivendale General Store as at 31 May 1976

	£		£	£
Sources of finance		*Assets*		
Proprietor's capital	35,000	*Fixed assets*		
		Premises	30,000	
Long-term liabilities		Furniture and		
Mortgage on premises	10,000	fittings	6,000	
				36,000
Current liabilities				
Trade creditors	1,500			
		Current assets		
		Stock-in-trade	7,000	
		Debtors	2,000	
		Bank	1,000	
		Cash	500	
				10,500
	46,500			46,500

ANSWER

I would say that the business was worth £35,000. Do you agree? If not you may have said £46,500 – the total value of the assets. This is incorrect because although the *assets* are worth £46,500, outsiders to the business are owed a total of £11,500 (the mortgage on the premises and trade creditors). Therefore when we take away from the assets an amount which is owing for the liabilities we are left with the net value of the business. This is the same as the value of the proprietor's capital: £35,000. In other words we have repeated a calculation based on the book-keeping equation.

assets less *liabilities* = *capital*

or *assets* less *liabilities* = *net value of business*.

I have made two assumptions in making this valuation:

- The assets are worth the value stated in the balance sheet. Of course, if the premises had not been revalued for a number of years the business might be worth considerably more. However, if the debtors' figure included debts which had been owing for a considerable time, they might never be collected and the business would be worth less.
- There is no goodwill to be purchased. If you have forgotten what this means, refer back to page 17.

An agreement to sell such a business could be made in a number of different ways. Provided the above assumptions are correct, however, the seller would expect to be £35,000 better off after it has been sold.

You may have noticed that the balance sheet in the above exercise contained more information than was shown in the opening balance sheet of Bill Turner's Valuemart on page 18. Take another look at both of them. First, concentrate on the assets side of the balance sheets.

You will notice that the assets in the second balance sheet are grouped into two sections: fixed assets and current assets. Fixed assets are those possessions which are relatively permanent. They are used over a reasonable amount of time and are not constantly changing in value. Fixed assets are needed to enable the business to operate and make a profit, but they are not kept with the set purpose of making a profit on them.

Self-check

If you understand this definition you should be able to think of some other examples of assets which might be termed 'fixed'. You do not have to keep to the sort of business used here.

ANSWER

Other typical fixed assets include vehicles, machinery, and equipment such as a computer or micro-processor.

Current assets are also sometimes known as 'circulating' assets. They are the assets which are constantly changing in value and it is through the movement of these that the proprietor of a business intends to make a profit. As more stock is bought so this asset increases in value. If it is sold then it decreases in value. At the same time, either the amount of cash in hand or cash at bank will be changing as the business receives money or makes payments.

One new asset appears in the Rivendale balance sheet. This is debtors. Clearly debtors are not a possession in the same sense as property or cash but it is an advantage on which a money value may be placed. It is an advantage because the majority of debtors do pay their debts. Since businesses normally expect their debtors to pay them relatively soon, it is regarded as a current rather than a fixed asset.

You should beware of thinking that all assets can be classified as either fixed or current and remain the same whatever business is involved. It is the *use* to which the asset is put which determines whether it should be regarded as fixed or current.

Self-check

Where would you place motorcars in the balance sheets of the following businesses? Are they fixed or current assets?

a The cars used by the salesmen of a confectionary firm.
b The cars on the forecourt of a garage with 'for sale' on each windscreen.

ANSWER

a These cars should be classified as fixed assets. They will last for a reasonable amount of time and, while they contribute to a firm's ability to make profits, it is not intended that profits should be made directly from any change in their value.
b These should be regarded as current assets. They are a means by which the garage is making a profit. Cars will be bought and sold and thus the value of this asset will often be changing. From the garage's point of view the cars will be part of their stock-in-trade, one of the things that they trade in.

The assets in the balance sheet of Rivendale have been displayed in order of permanence. The fixed assets are followed by the current assets. Property, which probably takes longer to turn into cash than any other asset, is shown first and cash comes last. This is the normal practice in the UK, though in some other countries the assets are shown in order of liquidity. Then cash comes first and those assets which can be turned into cash follow in the order of how quickly they can be turned into cash.

Self-check

If the assets were shown in order of liquidity, which group of assets would come first? Which individual asset would be last?

ANSWER

Current assets would be shown first as cash is a current asset. Property would come last among the fixed assets because this is the least liquid or most permanent asset.

Types of liabilities
Now compare the finance side of Rivendale's balance sheet with that of Bill Turner. You will see that the former contains two types of liabilities: long-term and current. Liabilities are finance

provided by people or other organisations who are not owners of the business. The money has to be repaid at some time. The distinction between long-term and current is usually made on the basis of the amount of time allowed to repay the amount due. A liability that is due to be repaid within one year is normally regarded as current. Trade creditors are the suppliers from whom Rivendale has purchased its stock-in-trade on credit. Usually suppliers will allow a maximum of only one or two months' credit before payment is demanded. Trade creditors must therefore be regarded as current liabilities. Liabilities which are not expected to be repaid during the current year, e.g. a mortgage, are regarded as long-term.

Self-check

Write down some other liabilities that a firm might have. Try to decide whether they are more likely to be long-term or current.

ANSWER

Long-term liabilities may include loans from banks or finance companies and hire-purchase debts. If you know anything about limited companies you may also have included debentures. These are long-term loans which are explained in *Practical Accounts 2* in the Pan Breakthrough series.

For current liabilities you might have included any expense creditors. These are other firms or people who have provided a service for which the business has not yet paid. Examples often include property rented to the firm, wages due to employees, cleaning and catering services. Until they are paid they are helping to finance the operation of the business and may be regarded as sources of finance. You might also have mentioned the government because, for a number of reasons, many firms do not pay their taxes on the due date. They are thus often in debt to the government.

Confusion often arises over bank overdrafts. Clearly this is money which the business owes to the bank. Should it be regarded as a long-term or current liability? The correct answer is current because a bank may recall this money on demand at any time. It is true that many firms are sometimes allowed by banks to keep their overdrafts over a relatively long period. This does not make them a long-term liability, however, because the owner of the business can never be *sure* that the bank might not demand immediate repayment. It is also possible for a bank loan to be regarded as current. This will depend on the terms agreed with the bank for repayment.

Before attempting the final exercise in this chapter, make certain that you understand each of the following: balance sheet, the book-keeping equation, proprietor's capital, long-term liabilities, current liabilities, fixed assets and current assets. Are you happy? If so, you should be able to answer the following.

Exercise

The information that follows refers to the business of Peter Bright on 31 January 1981: freehold property £40,000, debts due to suppliers £2,350, stock £6,800, cash £180, bank overdraft £1,000, debts due from customers £1,900, furniture and fittings £3,000, delivery vehicle £2,000, mortgage on property (10 years) £5,000, loan from ABC Finance Limited (5 years) £3,000.

Tasks

1 Draft a balance sheet for Peter Bright on the date given. *Advice*: take care to divide your assets and liabilities as you have been shown on page 22. To complete the balance sheet, you will need to calculate one piece of information which has been left out. Refer to the book-keeping equation for help.
2 Assuming that the assets and liabilities are correctly valued and that Peter has no goodwill, how much is the business worth to its owner?

ANSWERS

1 My solution looks like this:

Balance sheet of Peter Bright as at 31 January 1981

	£	£			£	£
Sources of finance			*Assets*			
Capital		42,530	*Fixed assets*			
			Freehold			
Long-term liabilities			property	40,000		
Mortgage	5,000		Furniture and			
ABC Finance Ltd	3,000		fittings	3,000		
	———		Delivery vehicle	2,000		
		8,000		———		
						45,000
			Current assets			
Current liabilities			Stock	6,800		
Trade creditors	2,350		Trade debtors	1,900		
Bank overdraft	1,000		Cash	180		
	———			———		
		3,350				8,880
		———				———
		53,880				53,880
		———				———

Compare this balance sheet with yours. The following notes should help you if there are differences.

- The heading is important. It tells us that this is the position of Peter Bright at a certain date, 31 January 1981.
- If your calculation of the total assets differs from mine, one or more of the following is likely:

   (a) You have confused debts due to suppliers with debts due from customers. The latter is an advantage to the business in that payment can be expected. It is therefore an asset and is usually written as 'debtors' or 'trade debtors'. The former is a liability because the business owes its suppliers money and will soon have to pay them.

   (b) You have included £1,000 as money in the bank. This is wrong because there is no money in the bank to be shown as an asset. In fact Peter Bright has overdrawn his current account by £1,000 and therefore owes this sum to the bank. It is a liability of the business.

(c)   You have made an error of addition.

- The assets are shown in order of permanence with fixed assets coming before current assets and cash (the only truly liquid asset) last of all.
- The mortgage and loan from ABC Finance Limited are not due for repayment in the current year and should be regarded as long-term.
- Trade creditors and bank overdraft are both current liabilities. The former is normally repayable within a month or so and the bank overdraft is repayable on demand if the bank manager so decides.
- Capital of the proprietor was the figure missing. It can be calculated by means of the book-keeping equation: total assets (£53,880) less total liabilities (£11,350) = capital (£42,530). However, you did not have to do a separate calculation to get this right. Provided all your other figures are correct, then £42,530 is the *only* figure which can be inserted to make the balance sheet balance. Remember the sources of finance must equal the value of the assets. I call this the jigsaw method. Capital was the only piece missing and it had to be the right size to give the picture its completeness.
- The sources of finance are also shown in order of permanence with the most permanent finance (the proprietor's capital) coming first and the least permanent (the bank overdraft) last. While this is not essential for the accuracy of the balance sheet, it does fit in better with the assets side. It is considered to be good style. For this reason also it is worth making certain that the totals of the two sides of the balance sheet end up level with each other.

2   Provided your balance sheet is now correct, you should have said £42,530. If you do not agree, reread pages 22–3.

We have now explored in a preliminary way the question: how much is that business worth? The next question might be: how much will that business be worth next week or next month? The answer to this won't be found in the above balance sheet, as we shall see in the next chapter.

Activity

Draft a balance sheet to show your own assets and liabilities. Remember to include only those which may easily be valued. Strength in a man, or a good figure in a woman, may be valuable assets in the general sense of that word. They are of no use, however, to the accountant!

3 | The balance sheet in action

Now that you understand what a balance sheet is, we are going to look at how it changes once a business begins operating.

Remind yourself of the position of Bill Turner's Valuemart (page 18) before he began trading. He has made at least two transactions already. First, he purchased the premises, fixtures and stock from the previous owner. Second, he borrowed £10,000 from the bank. Once trading begins the number of transactions will increase.

|| *Activity*

Make a list of transactions that Bill will be undertaking regularly from now on.

RESPONSE

My list includes selling his stock to customers, purchasing more stock from suppliers, making payments for insurances, heating, lighting and rates. He might purchase new equipment and perhaps negotiate for a further loan to pay for it. There are many more and it is important to realise that the people involved in successful businesses will be busy. They will be dealing with a variety of different transactions. Each time a transaction is made it will affect the business. Let's see how. To simplify things imagine that Bill begins very slowly making only one transaction a day at first.

On 2 July Bill purchased a new fridge for £300, paying for it by cheque. After this transaction his balance sheet would have looked like this:

Balance sheet of Valuemart as at 2 July 1976

	£		£
Owner's capital	22,000	Premises	26,000
Bank loan	10,000	Furniture and fittings	2,300
		Stock	2,000
		Bank	1,600
		Cash	100
	32,000		32,000

One asset, furniture and fittings, has increased in value by £300 while another, bank, has been reduced by the same amount. The balance sheet still balances and the totals are the same as at 1 July. Note, this balance sheet and the ones that follow have been simplified by omitting the division of assets into fixed and current and liabilities into long-term and current.

On 3 July, Bill purchased £500 worth of stock on credit from a supplier. His balance sheet again changed.

Balance sheet of Valuemart as at 3 July 1976

	£		£
Owner's capital	22,000	Premises	26,000
Bank loan	10,000	Furniture and fittings	2,300
Trade creditor	500	Stock	2,500
		Bank	1,600
		Cash	100
	32,500		32,500

This time an asset, stock, has increased by £500 while a new liability, trade creditors, has been increased by the same amount. The balance sheet still balances but this time with totals £500 more than on 2 July.

On 4 July, Bill sold an old fridge, which had been valued at £100 when he bought the business, to a friend for £100. His friend paid £50 in cash and agreed to pay the rest later. Bill's balance sheet then looked like this.

Balance sheet of Valuemart as at 4 July 1976

	£		£
Owner's capital	22,000	Premises	26,000
Bank loan	10,000	Furniture and fittings	2,200
Trade creditor	500	Stock	2,500
		Debtor	50
		Bank	1,600
		Cash	150
	32,500		32,500

On this occasion one asset, furniture and fittings, has been reduced by £100 while there has been an increase in cash of £50 and a new asset, debtor £50, is included. The net effect is that the assets are still worth what they were before the transaction and the balance sheet totals are unchanged.

Self-check

You should now be able to calculate the effect of the following transaction. Redraft the balance sheet and say what changes have taken place.

On 5 July, Bill saw an electronic till reduced to £500 in a sale. The seller would not allow credit and Bill did not want to use any of the money he had available. He managed to persuade his bank manager to lend him the £500 which he used at once to buy the till.

ANSWER

Balance sheet of Valuemart as at 5 July 1976

	£		£
Owner's capital	22,000	Premises	26,000
Bank loan	10,500	Furniture and fittings	2,700
Trade creditors	500	Stock	2,500
		Debtor	50
		Bank	1,600
		Cash	150
	33,000		33,000

His furniture and fittings have increased in value by £500, the value of the till, and the amount he owes to the bank has increased by the same amount. Thus the balance sheet totals £500 more on each side.

On 6 July, Bill started selling and that day he did very well. He sold £300 worth of stock for £400. How did this affect his balance sheet? His stock was reduced in value by £300 but his cash increased by £400. It seems, on first thought, that the balance sheet would not then balance because the assets had increased by £100. However, it must be realised that this £100 represents Bill's profit to date. It is shown in the balance sheet by adding it to his capital. It is extra finance for him to use as he wishes. The balance sheet would now look like this:

Balance sheet of Valuemart as at 6 July 1976

	£		£
Owner's capital	22,000	Premises	26,000
add Profit	100	Furniture and fittings	2,700
	———	Stock	2,200
	22,100	Debtor	50
Bank loan	10,500	Bank	1,600
Trade creditors	500	Cash	550
	———		———
	33,100		33,100

To see if you can keep track of the changes resulting from a series of transactions, attempt the following:

Exercise

On 1 February 1982 Tom Spear decided to start a mobile greengrocery business. He opened a business bank account with £2,000 of his own money and his balance sheet looked like this:

Balance sheet of Tom Spear as at 1 Feb. 1982

	£		£
Capital	2,000	Bank	2,000

During the next week he made the following transactions:

2 Feb. Negotiated a loan of £500 with his bank manager which was paid into his bank account.

3 Feb. Purchased a motor vehicle for £2,200 from ACE Motors. He paid £1,600 by cheque and agreed to pay the balance within three months.

4 Feb. Withdrew £50 from the bank for use as cash.

5 Feb. Purchased £200 worth of fruit and vegetables, paying for them by cheque.

6 Feb. On his first day of selling he received £120 cash for the sale of £80 worth of fruit and vegetables.

Show his balance sheet on 6 Feb. after all these transactions had taken place. It may help you to do a balance sheet after each transaction.

ANSWER

I will go through each transaction in turn.

2 Feb. Asset, bank + £500; liability, bank loan + £500.

Balance sheet of Tom Spear as at 2 Feb. 1982

	£		£
Capital	2,000	Bank	2,500
Bank loan	500		
	2,500		2,500

3 Feb. Asset, motor vehicle + £2,200; asset, bank − £1,600; liability ACE Motors + £600.

Balance sheet of Tom Spear as at 3 Feb. 1982

	£		£
Capital	2,000	Motor vehicles	2,200
Bank loan	500	Bank	900
Creditor, ACE Motors	600		
	3,100		3,100

4 Feb. Asset, bank − £50; asset, cash + £50.

Balance sheet of Tom Spear as at 4 Feb. 1982

	£		£
Capital	2,000	Motor vehicle	2,200
Bank loan	500	Bank	850
Creditor, ACE Motors	600	Cash	50
	3,100		3,100

5 Feb. Asset, stock + £200 (the term 'stock' is given to the asset which is bought and sold to make a profit); asset, bank − £200.

Balance sheet of Tom Spear as at 5 Feb. 1982

	£		£
Capital	2,000	Motor vehicle	2,200
Bank loan	500	Stock	200
Creditor, ACE Motors	600	Bank	650
		Cash	50
	3,100		3,100

6 Feb. Asset, stock − £80; asset, cash + £120; owner's capital + £40 (the latter is the profit which belongs to the owner).

Balance sheet of Tom Spear as at 6 Feb. 1982

	£		£
Capital	2,000	Motor vehicle	2,200
add Profit	40	Stock	120
	———	Bank	650
	2,040	Cash	170
Bank loan	500		
Creditor, ACE Motors	600		
	———		———
	3,140		3,140

Of course in most businesses transactions will be taking place with much greater frequency than in the above exercise. There will also be a much greater variety of transactions. This variety will be most evident in businesses which are expanding or already have interests in a range of different activities. Reflect for a moment on this question. How suitable is the balance sheet as a means of recording the large number of different transactions that are taking place continuously?

Some thought should lead you to the conclusion that it is not at all suitable. For a businessman to rewrite his balance sheet after each transaction or even after each week's transactions would be quite time-consuming. In addition it would not provide enough information about the actual transactions. Some other method is needed, therefore, and this will form the subject matter of the next chapter.

If the balance sheet is so unsuited to reflecting day-to-day changes, why have we used it in that way in this chapter? The answer to my question is that it is an excellent way of learning that:

- every transaction affects a business by altering either the assets or sources of finance or both, while
- the fundamental relationship between sources of finance and assets does not alter.

Understanding these points is central to understanding accounting.

Review

1 Complete the following statement: Any transaction causes at least _____ changes within the balance sheet. As a result of these changes the total value of the _____ will still equal the value of _____ of _____.

2 Write down the book-keeping equation on which the balance sheet is based.

3 Explain what happens to the items in the book-keeping equation when £200 worth of unfashionable stock is reduced and sold for £120 cash.

4 Look back at the balance sheet of Valuemart as at 6 July on page 34 and rewrite it in good style. Assume that the bank loan does not have to be repaid for five years.

ANSWERS

1 The missing words in order are: two, assets, sources, finance.
2 Capital + liabilities = assets.
3 Stock is reduced by £200 and cash is increased by £120 thus the total value of assets is reduced by £80. This £80 represents a loss which is borne by the owner of the business and is deducted from his capital. Thus the sources of finance are also reduced by £80.

If this caused difficulty, reread Bill's transaction of 6 July on page 34. He made a profit which was added to his capital. A loss, the opposite of profit, is shown by deducting it from the owner's capital.

4 Your balance sheet should have subtotals of £28,700 for fixed assets and £4,400 for current assets. The bank loan should be shown as a long-term liability and trade creditors as a current liability. In this chapter we have been more concerned with the changes taking place within a balance sheet than with its layout. However, the latter must not be forgotten. Return to the example on page 22 for help if necessary.

4 | Double entry book-keeping

The last chapter demonstrated how any transaction will have two effects on a balance sheet. You should now be able to identify which assets and/or sources of finance are affected by different transactions. In this chapter I will introduce a more efficient way of recording transactions than redrafting a balance sheet after each one. This will be done by means of ledger accounts. You will learn the principles of double entry book-keeping which will enable you to keep a simple set of ledger accounts.

Book-keeping is the part of accounting concerned with recording transactions. The main book used to record these transactions is known as the ledger. At one time all ledgers were bound volumes. Today loose-leaf paper, ledger cards and computer-based systems are used. Whatever the means used to record transactions, the principles and methods are basically the same.

The ledger contains accounts of each asset and liability of the business as well as the capital of the owner. It also contains other types of account which will be introduced in the next chapter. The word 'account' is usually abbreviated to 'a/c' and means 'a record of'. Each account contains a record of changes in one particular asset, liability or in the capital. Overleaf is the traditional layout of a page in the ledger.

Note:

- Each page in the ledger is divided clearly into two sides.
- The left-hand side is known as the debit side but is usually abbreviated to 'Dr'. This abbreviation derives from 'Debtor', a term still used in some texts to describe the left-hand side of the page.

4

Dr						Cash account				Cr
date	details	folio	£	p	date	details	folio	£	p	

- The right-hand side is known as the credit side and is abbreviated to 'Cr'. The word 'credit' has different meanings in other contexts. When referring to ledger accounts, though, it is simply the right-hand side of the account.
- The name of the account is written at the top of the page, which is numbered for reference purposes. The cash a/c above is on page 4 of the ledger. Some accounts will require more pages than others. The loose-leaf system provides useful flexibility in such circumstances.
- The columns on the debit side are the same as on the credit side. There is space to record the date, brief details and the amount of money involved in a transaction. The folio column is used mainly to provide a cross-reference system. This will be demonstrated later.

Ledger paper and books can be purchased from all good stationers.

Self-check

A businessman keeps a record of his motor vehicles on page 22 of his ledger. Draft an outline for this account, labelling the columns correctly.

ANSWER

Apart from the name (motor vehicles account) and the page number (22), your outline should be the same as in my example above. Did you label it correctly? It is especially important to remember that the debit (Dr) is on the left-hand side of the page and credit (Cr) on the right-hand side. This causes problems to those who find difficulty in distinguishing right from left. One student solved the problem by thinking of the debit side as the side of the room on which the door was situated. Much more logical, he thought, especially as Dr is seen more easily as short for door. One day, however, his class was moved to another room in which the door was on the right-hand side of the room. You can imagine the effect on his work! There is no real substitute for learning that the debit side is to the left and the credit side is to the right of a ledger account.

Let's turn now to the principles and practice of keeping a ledger. Suppose that Bill Turner, to whom we referred in Chapters 2 and 3, decided when he started the business that he would keep a set of ledger accounts. How should he begin? One way is to write down the state of the business on the date he decides to begin his ledger. The easiest way of showing this clearly is by means of a balance sheet. Bill's balance sheet of 1 July 1976 is repeated here for ease of reference.

Balance sheet of Valuemart as at 1 July 1976

	£		£
Sources of finance		*Assets*	
Owner's capital	22,000	Premises	26,000
		Furniture and fittings	2,000
Liabilities		Stock	2,000
Bank loan	10,000	Bank	1,900
		Cash	100
	32,000		32,000

The first step is to open a ledger account for each item in the balance sheet. The value of each asset is placed on the debit side of its own account, while the values of capital and any liabilities are placed on the credit side of their accounts. The date will be that of the balance sheet from which we have taken the figures and in the details column each entry can be described by the term 'balance'. For the time being we will not bother giving each account a page number as the use of the folio column for cross-referencing will be dealt with later. Apart from the fact that they wouldn't be condensed together on one page, the ledger accounts will then appear as opposite.

One thing that causes people concern at this stage is that the assets and sources of finance have changed sides. In the balance sheet assets are shown on the right and sources of finance – capital and liabilities – on the left. Now that we have opened ledger accounts, however, the assets are shown as debit balances, on the left of their accounts, and sources of finance are shown as credit balances, on the right of their own accounts. Don't be alarmed! The balance sheet is not part of the ledger. It could be, and often is, written in other ways. For example the sources of finance could be written beneath the assets in a vertical list rather than placed to the left-hand side of them. The important thing to learn is that asset values are shown as debit balances while sources of finance are shown as credit balances. This convention *must* be followed, whereas the balance sheet can be written in a number of different ways.

Self-check

What is the relationship between the total value of debit balances and credit balances in the accounts of Valuemart on 1 July?

ANSWER

The debit balances exactly equal the credit balances. You probably said this without having to add them up. In Chapter 1 you learnt that a balance sheet was a reflection of the book-keeping equation: capital + liabilities = assets. If all the assets are now entered on the debit side of their ledger accounts while the capital and liabilities are placed on the credit side of their accounts, it follows that the total value of all the debit balances must equal the total value of all the credit balances.

The next step in keeping a ledger is to enter transactions in the accounts. We will consider the assets first and then the sources of finance. An asset is represented in its own account by a debit

Dr		Premises account			Cr
1976		£			£
1 July	Balance	26,000.00			

		Furniture and fittings account			
1 July	Balance	2,000.00			

		Stock account			
1 July	Balance	2,000.00			

		Bank account			
1 July	Balance	1,900.00			

		Cash account			
1 July	Balance	100.00			

		Capital account			
			1 July	Balance	22,000.00

		Bank loan account			
			1 July	Balance	10,000.00

balance. If something happens to increase the value of this asset, we show it by making another debit entry. If the asset is reduced in value a credit entry is made in that account.

For example, on 1 May, Tom Smith possessed two delivery vehicles worth £4,000 and £2,000. On 2 May he purchased another for £1,000 and 3 May he sold his most valuable vehicle for £4,000, exactly what it was worth. These events would be recorded as follows.

Dr			Delivery vehicles account	Cr
		£		£
1 May	Balance	6,000	3 May	4,000
2 May		1,000		

Self-check

From the account state the value of Tom's delivery vehicles at the end of transactions on **a** 1 May, **b** 2 May, **c** 3 May.

ANSWER

a £6,000 – this represents the two vehicles worth £4,000 and £2,000.

b £7,000 – he has purchased another vehicle for £1,000 and has not yet sold any. The only entries in the delivery account on 2 May will be the two debit entries. The debit entry for £1,000 increases the value of this asset by that amount.

c £3,000 – selling the vehicle worth £4,000 for that amount reduces the value of his delivery vehicles. The credit entry for £4,000 reduces the value of this asset by that amount.

Sources of finance, whether owner's capital or liabilities to outsiders, are shown in their own accounts by credit balances. If something happens to increase the value of one of these, we show it by making another credit entry. If the source of finance is reduced in value a debit entry is made in that account.

For example, on 1 May, Tom Smith owed Busifinance Co. £4,000, which had been borrowed to enable him to start his business. On 4 May he negotiated a further loan of £3,000 but on 8 May an early and successful conclusion of a deal enabled him to repay £2,000. These events in the account of this liability will be recorded as follows.

Dr		Busifinance Co. account		Cr
	£			£
8 May	2,000	1 May	Balance	4,000
		4 May		3,000

Self-check

From the account state the amount owed by Tom to Busifinance Co. at the end of transactions on **a** 1 May, **b** 4 May, **c** 8 May.

ANSWER

a £4,000 – the original sum borrowed.
b £7,000 – he has borrowed a further £3,000. The only entries in the account on 4 May will be the two credit entries. The credit entry for £3,000 increases the liability by that amount.
c £5,000 – repaying £2,000 reduces the amount owing. The debit entry for £2,000 enables this to be shown in the account.

What has been learnt so far about entries in ledger accounts can be summarised for easy reference.

Debit	Any asset account	Credit
1 Opening value of that asset. 2 Increases in value of that asset.		Deductions in value of that asset.

Debit	Any source of finance account	Credit
Deductions in value of that source of finance.		1 Opening value of that source of finance. 2 Increase in value of that source of finance.

The amount that any asset is worth can be calculated at any time. If the original value of an asset together with any additions to it are on the debit side and deductions are on the credit side, the difference between the two sides on a certain date will tell us what the asset is then worth. Similarly, the amount of a liability or the owner's capital can be calculated. If the original value of a source of finance together with any additions to it are on the credit side and deductions are on the debit side, the difference between the two sides at a particular time will tell us the amount of the liability or capital at that time.

When considering the effect of transactions on the balance sheet in Chapter 3 we saw how every transaction caused two changes in the assets and/or sources of finance of the business. This is shown in the ledger by making two entries, one in each account affected. Double entry book-keeping is the name given to this system of recording transactions in the ledger. It is important that you learn how to operate it.

As an example, look back at Tom Smith's delivery vehicles account on page 44. Neither the transaction of 2 May nor that of 3 May have any description in the 'details' column. This is because I did not give enough information for it to be completed. Take the transaction of 2 May – Tom purchased a vehicle for £1,000. How did he purchase it? There are two possibilities. First he could have paid for it at the time of purchase. If he did this, besides showing an increase in his delivery vehicles by debiting this account, we should also show a reduction in one of his money accounts for the same amount. Whether this would involve an entry in the cash account or the bank account would depend on whether he paid by cash or by cheque. Let's assume he paid such a large sum by cheque. What kind of entry would you have to make in the bank account?

If you said credit, good. If not look at the summary on page 45 again. A deduction from an asset is shown by a credit entry in that account. Clearly the money in Tom's bank account would go down as a result of paying £1,000 by cheque for a vehicle. Therefore the bank account should be credited. (Those readers with current bank accounts who receive bank statements might find this confusing. When you pay £1,000 for, say, a vehicle the bank will debit your account. This is because they are looking at the transaction from their point of view, not yours. If you have money in a current bank account, the bank owes you the money. From their point of view this is a liability. When you use £1,000 of it to pay someone, the bank owes you less. They show this reduction of the liability by a debit entry. We will look at this in more detail in Chapter 9).

In double entry book-keeping each entry is described by the name of the account affected. The description in the details column of Tom's delivery vehicles account would therefore be 'bank'. In his bank account the description would be 'delivery vehicles'.

A second possibility is that Tom did not pay for the vehicle at the time of purchase but agreed to pay at a later date. This is known as a credit purchase. In this case the other effect of the purchase is that he owes £1,000 to the seller. This is a liability to Tom. The seller was Ted's Garage. An account would have to be opened for this company if one did not already exist. What kind of entry would it be? If you said credit, good. If not, look again at the summary on page 45. An increase or the start of a liability is shown by a credit entry in that account. Clearly Tom owes £1,000 to Ted's Garage as a result of this transaction, therefore the account for Ted's Garage should be credited.

Self-check

If Tom did obtain the vehicle on credit from Ted's Garage, what would the descriptions in the details column of the two accounts affected be?

ANSWER

In the delivery vehicles account the description would be 'Ted's Garage' and in the account for Ted's Garage the description would be 'delivery vehicles'. Remember, in double-entry book-keeping an entry is described by the name of the other account affected.

Of course, it is also possible that Tom might have combined the above two methods of purchase. He could have paid a deposit of, say, £400 by cheque and agreed to pay the outstanding £600 at a later date. If this was the case there would be a credit entry of only £400 in the bank account showing a reduction in this asset by that amount. There would also be a credit entry of £600 in the account for Ted's Garage, showing a liability of that amount. How would this be shown in the delivery vehicles account? The easiest way is to make two debit entries on the same date – one for £400 described as 'bank' and the other for £600 described as 'Ted's Garage'.

Tom's transaction of 2 May, however it was financed, illustrates the most important principle of double-entry bookkeeping:

● *Every transaction involves a debit entry in one account and a corresponding credit entry in another account.*

If a transaction is more complicated it may involve two debit entries in one account and two separate credit entries in different accounts. The value of the debit entry or entries for each transaction, however, must equal the value of the credit entry or entries. This is how we express in the ledger what was learnt earlier when observing the effect of transactions on the balance sheet. Every transaction has two effects on the assets and/or sources of finance. In the ledger every transaction involves a debit entry in one account and a corresponding credit entry in another account.

Self-check

Look again at Tom's delivery vehicles account on page 44. The entry on 3 May shows a reduction in the vehicles by £4,000 – the value of the one sold on that date. What kind of entry will be needed to complete the recording of this transaction?

ANSWER

Debit. The entry in delivery vehicles account is a credit entry. For each transaction there must be a debit entry to correspond to each credit entry.

Exercise

Referring again to Tom's transaction of 3 May, draft Tom's ledger accounts and complete the entries for each of the following separate possibilities:

a Tom sold the vehicle for £4,000 cash.
b Tom sold the vehicle to Parkhill Motors on credit.
c Parkhill Motors paid £1,000 by cheque and agreed to pay the outstanding £3,000 at a later date.

ANSWER

a

Delivery vehicles account	Cr	Dr	Cash account
	3 May Cash £4,000	3 May Delivery vehicles £4,000	

The credit entry in delivery vehicles account shows the reduction in the value of an asset. The debit entry in cash account shows a corresponding increase in another asset.

b

Delivery vehicles account	Cr	Dr	Parkhill Motors account
	3 May Parkhill Motors £4,000	3 May Delivery vehicles £4,000	

The credit entry in delivery vehicles account shows the reduction in the value of that asset. The debit entry in the account for Parkhill Motors shows another asset increasing by the same amount. Note that selling on credit means the purchaser owes money to Tom. The purchaser is therefore a debtor to Tom. Debtors like Parkhill Motors are assets because it is expected that debtors will pay their debts.

c

Delivery vehicles account		Cr	Dr	Parkhill Motors account	
	3 May Parkhill			3 May Delivery	
	Motors	£3,000		vehicles	£3,000
	3 May Bank	£1,000			

Dr	Bank account		Cr
3 May Delivery vehicles	£1,000		

This time three accounts are affected. However, the total
debit entries still equal the total credit entries. The credit
entries in delivery vehicles account reduce the value of the
asset by £4,000. The debit entry in the bank account shows an
increase in this asset by £1,000. The debit entry in the account
for Parkhill Motors shows that the remaining £3,000 is owed to
Tom by that garage. This is also an asset to Tom.

Note that whichever of the above circumstances applies
there is a debit entry for each credit entry. Also the description
of each account is the name of the other account affected by
the transaction.

Understanding double-entry book-keeping is important. If you
follow what we have done in this chapter so far, fine. If not, you
should look through it again before attempting the following
exercise. Practising it is the best way to master double-entry
book-keeping.

Exercise

On page 43 in this chapter I opened a set of ledger accounts
for Bill Turner's Valuemart, which began business on 1
July 1976. Copy out these accounts leaving space to enter
these transactions:

2 July Bill purchased a new fridge for £300, by cheque.
3 July He purchased £500 worth of stock on credit from a supplier called JLK Foods.

4 July He sold an old fridge worth £100 to a friend, Sally Moore, for that amount. She paid £50 in cash and agreed to pay the rest later.

5 July He borrowed a further £500 from his bank and used it to buy an electronic till.

6 July He sold £300 worth of stock for £400 cash.

These are the transactions we used in Chapter 3. They have been repeated for your convenience. Complete the entries for each of the transactions, opening new accounts where necessary. Make certain that every transaction has a debit entry to correspond to each credit entry.

ANSWER

Dr			Premises account			Cr
1976		£		*1976*		£
1 July	Balance	26,000.00				

		Furniture and fittings account				
1 July	Balance	2,000.00	4 July	S. Moore		50.00
2 July	Bank	300.00	4 July	Cash		50.00
5 July	Bank loan	500.00				

		Stock account				
1 July	Balance	2,000.00	6 July	Cash		300.00
3 July	JLK	500.00				

		Bank account				
1 July	Balance	1,900.00	2 July	Furniture and fittings		300.00

		Cash account				
1 July	Balance	100.00				
4 July	Furniture and fittings	50.00				
6 July	Stock	300.00				
6 July	Owner's capital	100.00				

Dr	Capital account		Cr
£			£
	1 July	Balance	22,000.00
	6 July	Cash	100.00

	Bank loan account		
	1 July	Balance	10,000.00
	5 July	Furniture and fittings	500.00

	S. Moore account		
4 July	Furniture and fittings	50.00	

	JLK account		
	3 July	Stock	500.00

If for each transaction you made certain that the value of the debit entry or entries equalled the value of the credit entry or entries, your solution should be similar to mine. Check through this solution, taking the transactions one at a time. Any difficulties you encountered probably occurred with the transactions of 4 July and 6 July.

On 4 July we have to show a reduction of £100 worth of furniture and fittings. As £50 is received in cash and £50 remains owing from Sally Moore there are two debit entries. The easiest way to show the reduction in furniture and fittings is to make two separate entries in this account as shown. Note that some owners may keep one single account for all their debtors, called sundry debtors' account, rather than a separate one for each as I have done here.

On 6 July cash had increased by £400, therefore the cash account has to be debited with this amount. However, we credit the stock account with only £300 since this is the actual worth of the stock sold. The remaining £100 is the profit on the deal and belongs to the owner. Therefore this is credited to his capital account. The simplest way of recording this transaction is by making two debits in the cash account – one for each of the separate credits.

Review

1 Define the terms 'account', 'ledger' and 'double entry book-keeping'.
2 Imagine you are about to open a ledger and that you have an up-to-date balance sheet. On which side of their accounts will you enter **a** assets, **b** liabilities, **c** capital?
3 For an asset, what kind of entry shows **a** an increase and **b** a decrease in value?
4 For capital and liabilities, what kind of entry shows **a** an increase and **b** a decrease in value?

ANSWERS

1 An account is a record of an aspect of a business. The ledger is the main book used to record transactions. Double entry book-keeping is the system whereby for each debit entry there is a corresponding credit entry.
2 **a** Debit, **b** and **c** credit.
3 **a** Debit, **b** credit.
4 **a** Credit, **b** debit.

If you experienced difficulty with these questions, then you probably need to look through this chapter again. I cannot emphasise enough the importance of mastering the rules of double-entry book-keeping.

5 | Expanding the ledger

The last chapter introduced the principles of double-entry book-keeping and applied them to assets and sources of finance. In this chapter we will apply these rules to the asset, stock. Then we will consider how to deal with transactions involving expenses and incomes.

Many businesses are involved in buying and selling. The stock accounts of these businesses are therefore going to be very busy indeed, with large numbers of transactions to be entered. To keep things simple, four additional accounts are used to record the different events that change the amount of stock. These are: purchases account, purchases returns account, sales account and sales returns account. They may be thought of as subdivisions of the stock account.

Purchases

Purchases of stock increase the value of this asset. What kind of entry in the stock account shows this? If you have mastered the rules in the last chapter, you should have said 'debit'. Instead of making the debit entries in the stock account, we are going to enter all such debits in a purchases of stock account, which for convenience will be called the purchases account.

In which account will the corresponding credit entry be found? This will depend on the method of payment. If payment is made immediately the credit will be entered in the cash or bank accounts, showing the reduction of an asset. If the goods (as stock is sometimes called) are bought on credit then the credit will be entered in the account of the supplier, who is a creditor to the purchaser. This shows the increase of a liability.

Self-check

On 1 April a greengrocer bought £150 of fruit on credit from Fruitgrowers Ltd. Show the entries in the green-grocer's ledger accounts.

ANSWER

Dr	Purchases	Fruitgrowers Ltd	Cr
	£		£
1 April Fruitgrowers 150		1 April Purchases 150	

If you made an error, reread the above explanation.

Purchases returns

Sometimes goods which have been bought are later returned by the purchaser. This usually happens when something is found to be wrong with them. These purchases returns are also known as returns outward because they are being sent out from the firm which bought them. Sometimes, therefore, the account is called the returns outward account.

Let's see how such events are recorded in the purchaser's accounts. Suppose that the greengrocer mentioned above dis-covered that £20 worth of the fruit he had purchased was rotten. On 2 April he sent it back to the supplier. The real value of his purchases on 1 April is now £130 (£150 less £20 returned). Also he owes Fruitgrowers Ltd only £130. We can show the reduction of the liability by making a debit entry in the supplier's account, following the rules of the last chapter. The credit entry could be entered in the purchase account as this would achieve the desired effect of reducing the purchases figure to the right amount. To avoid complicating the purchases account, however, we make the credit entry in the purchases returns account. The accounts will now look like this:

Dr		Purchases			Cr
		£			£
1 April	Fruitgrowers	150			

		Fruitgrowers Ltd			
2 April	Purchases returns	20	1 April	Purchases	150

		Purchases returns			
			2 April	Fruitgrowers	20

The account for Fruitgrowers shows that £130 is now owing. To obtain the real value of the purchases we have to look at both the purchases account and the purchases returns account. Together they show that the net value of purchases is £130 (£150 less £20).

If all purchases and returns of goods bought were entered in the stock account the type of entries would be the same, i.e. a debit entry to record an increase of stock when goods are bought and a credit entry to show a reduction of stock when goods are returned. Putting all purchases of stock in the purchases account and purchases returns in a separate account helps keep things simple.

Sales

Sales of stock decrease the value of this asset. What kind of entry in the stock account would show this? Knowledge of the rules of entry introduced in Chapter 4 should have enabled you to say 'credit', which is the correct answer. Instead of making the credit entries in the stock account, however, we are going to make all such entres in the sales of stock account.

In which account will the corresponding debit entry be made? This will depend on how the stock was sold. If sold for money, it will be in either the cash or bank account, showing an increase in the value of one of these assets. If the goods were sold on credit then the person to whom they were sold owes that sum to the business. A debit entry in the customer's account will represent an asset because we assume that debtors will pay their debts.

Self-check

On 1 June a wholesaler sold £90 worth of tinned peas to Les Solt, a retailer who was allowed monthly credit. Show the entries in the wholesaler's accounts.

ANSWER

Sales		Cr	Dr		Les Solt	
		£			£	
1 June	L. Solt	90	1 June	Sales	90	

If you made an error, reread the above explanation.

Sales returns

When goods which have been sold are returned later for a valid reason, entries must be made to record the event. These sales returns are called returns inward because they are being returned back into stock by a customer. Sometimes, therefore, the account is known as the returns inward account.

Let's see how such a transaction is recorded in the seller's books. Suppose that, on checking the peas he had purchased, Mr Solt found that £10 worth of them were beans. As he had more than enough of these already he returned them to his supplier on 2 June. The wholesaler will have to reduce the amount of Solt's debt by £10. A credit entry will be made in Solt's account, following the rules in the last chapter. Remember, a debtor's account represents an asset and an asset is reduced by a credit entry. The corresponding debit entry for £10 could be made in the sales account, as this would have the desired effect of reducing the sales to its true figure. To avoid complicating the sales account, however, we make the debit entry in the sales returns account instead. The accounts will now look like this:

Dr		Sales		Cr
	£			£
		1 June	L. Solt	90

		Les Solt		
1 June	Sales	90	2 June Sales returns	10

		Sales returns		
2 June	L. Solt	10		

The account for Les Solt shows that £80 is now owed by him to the wholesaler. To obtain the real value of sales we have to look at both the sales account and the sales returns account. Together they show that the net value of the sales is £80 (£90 less £10).

If all sales and sales returns were entered in the stock account, the type of entries would be the same, i.e. a credit entry to record a decrease of stock when goods are sold and a debit entry to show an increase when goods are returned. Using a sales account to record all the sales and a separate sales returns account for all such returns helps to keep matters simple.

Correctly used the four accounts we have just considered enable the stock account to be reserved for the valuation of stock which is made at stocktaking time.

Self-check

1 State whether the entries in the following accounts will be debit or credit: **a** purchases, **b** purchases returns, **c** sales, **d** sales returns.
2 Give the alternative names for: **a** purchases returns, **b** sales returns.

ANSWERS

1 a Debit, **b** credit, **c** credit, **d** debit.
2 a Returns outward, **b** returns inward.

If this caused you no difficulty you should be able to deal with the following exercise. If it did, you should read from the start of this chapter again.

Exercise

Powa Electrics is a wholesaler which has Jim Hogg, a DIY retailer, as one of its customers. On 1 March, Jim owed £160 from the previous month. The following transactions then took place. On 2 March, Powa Electrics supplied Jim with £170 worth of materials on credit. On 3 March, Jim returned materials worth £40 because they were not of the type he had ordered.

Show how the above would be recorded in the ledger of **a** Powa Electrics and **b** Jim Hogg.

Note: when you do this kind of exercise it is important to be absolutely clear from whose point of view you are considering the transaction. Begin by labelling clearly for **a** *Powa Electrics books*. Then consider the transactions *solely* from this company's point of view. When you have done this put a new heading and consider the transactions from Jim Hogg's viewpoint.

ANSWER

a *Powa Electrics books*

Dr			Jim Hogg		Cr
		£			£
1 March	Balance	160	3 March	Sales returns	40
2 March	Sales	170			

	Sales		
			£
	2 March	Jim Hogg	170

	Sales returns	
3 March	Jim Hogg	40

It is most important to begin correctly. Powa Electrics will have an account for Jim Hogg as he is their customer. It will have a debit balance on 1 March showing that the £160 owing from the last month is an asset. The sale on 2 March increases the asset and the return on 3 March reduces it. The other accounts affected are sales, because Powa sold Jim goods, and sales returns, because part of what had been sold was returned.

b *Jim Hogg's books*

Dr		Powa Electrics			Cr
		£			£
3 March	Purchases	40	1 March	Balance	160
	Returns		2 March	Purchases	170

	Purchases	
2 March	Powa	170

	Purchases returns		
		3 March Powa	40

Jim Hogg won't have an account with his own name on it but he will have one for Powa Electrics because they are his suppliers. It starts with a credit balance showing that, from Jim's point of view, there is a liability of £160 on 1 March. The transaction of 2 March was a purchase as far as Jim is concerned and increases the amount he owes by £170. When he makes the return on 3 March, however, he owes Powa £40 less and is able to show the reduction of the liability by making a debit entry. The other accounts affected are purchases, because Jim bought the goods, and purchases returns, because a part of what he purchased has been sent back to the supplier.

So far all the transactions we have looked at have involved assets or sources of finance. We are now going to consider transactions that require other types of account as well.

Expenses

All businesses will have to make payments for a number of benefits and services they receive but which do not directly provide an asset owned by the business. These are known as expenses. For example the owner may employ people to work for him. In return for their services he will pay them wages or salaries depending on their conditions of service. He will need to open an account to record the amount they are paid. This will be called the wages or salaries account. Of course some employees may be wage earners and others salaried. In this case the business will usually have two separate accounts.

Activity

Make a list of some services required and expenses incurred by any business known to you.

RESPONSE

Services required by different businesses will vary but many will be the same. Some of the most common are: the use of another's property, for which rent will be paid; use of local authority services such as refuse collection and water provision, for which rates will be paid; the use of the Royal Mail, for which postage will be paid; and the use of a loan from someone else, on which interest will be paid. Each of these will be given its own account with a name which concisely explains its function. Accounts for the above services would be entitled 'rent', 'rates', 'postage' and 'interest on loan'. Other expenses you might have mentioned include: lighting and heating, advertising, repairs, insurance, telephone, carriage inwards (the delivery charge on goods coming into the firm, i.e. purchases) and carriage outwards (the delivery charge paid to have goods going out of the firm, i.e. sales).

The actual name given sometimes varies. For example, 'electricity account' may be preferred to 'lighting and heating account'. Some firms join similar expenses together such as rent and rates or postage and telephone. Small items may be put together under the heading 'sundry expenses', particularly if they do not occur often.

You may be able to work out what sort of entry will be needed in an expense account. Assume that a businessman who rents his premises makes his payments in cash. What sort of entry will he make in his cash account? Credit is the correct answer because this reduces the value of an asset. Each time the rent is paid, cash is reduced.

What sort of entry must be made, therefore, in the rent account? The answer must be debit because each transaction needs a debit and a credit entry. This does not give a reasoned explanation, but of course there is one. Expenses have been defined earlier as payments for services that do not directly provide an asset owned by the business. These services are advantages to the business, however, and very similar to assets in that respect. Therefore the rules for their entry are the same as for assets – a debit entry to record an increase and a credit entry to record a reduction in its own account. In the above example, each time the rent is paid the total amount paid is increased and therefore a debit entry is needed in the rent account.

Self-check

Complete the following table:

Transaction	Account to be debited	Account to be credited
a Paid wages by cash		
b Paid insurance by cheque		
c Received by cheque rebate of insurance previously paid		

ANSWER

Transaction	Dr	Cr
a Paid wages by cash	Wages	Cash
b Paid insurance by cheque	Insurance	Bank
c Received by cheque rebate of insurance previously paid	Bank	Insurance

Parts **a** and **b** should not have caused you any trouble. Both involve a credit entry to show a reduction in an asset account when payment is made and a debit in the expense account. Part **c** is less usual. Here the expense of insurance previously recorded by a debit in the insurance account must be reduced by the amount of the rebate. A credit entry is used to show this in the same way as a credit entry would be used to show the reduction of an asset. The corresponding debit entry will be made in the bank account because a cheque has been received and this will increase that asset.

We can summarise the rules for making entries in expense accounts as follows:

Debit	Any expense account	Credit
Increase of the expense		Decrease of the expense

The double entry will normally be completed by an entry in the cash or bank account. There are three main exceptions to this:

Discount allowed

This is an expense which many firms incur in order to encourage prompt payment from their debtors. For example, a retailer called Ben Wilson owed a wholesaler £200 for a purchase made on 18 May. In the wholesaler's books the debt will appear like this:

Dr	B. Wilson		Cr
		£	
18 May Sales		200	

The wholesaler has a policy of allowing debtors to deduct a discount of 3% for settlement within seven days of a statement being sent. This was done on 31 May and Wilson paid by cheque on 4 June. How much did he pay?

Wilson's cheque would have been for £194 as he is entitled to deduct £6 discount from the £200 due. Being able to calculate percentages is essential. I will explain the basic method in case you have forgotten it.

'Per cent' means per hundred. Whatever percentage is involved is written as a fraction of 100. Three per cent is therefore written $^3/_{100}$. The next step is to multiply this figure by the amount you are calculating the percentage of. In the above example this will be:

$$\frac{3}{100} \times \frac{200}{1} = £6.$$

The calculation can be done by calculator but it is important that you understand the principle of what you are doing.

Self-check

Calculate the amount of discount which could be deducted under the following circumstances:

Amount due £	Percentage discount
a 500	2
b 70	2
c 215	4

ANSWER

a

$$\frac{2}{100} \times \frac{500}{1} = £10.$$

b

$$\frac{2}{100} \times \frac{70}{1} = £1.40.$$

c

$$\frac{4}{100} \times \frac{215}{1} = £8.60.$$

If you made an error check that your figures were arranged as in the above solution.

Let's now return to the question of how the discount allowed to B. Wilson will be shown in the wholesaler's ledger. On 4 June two separate credit entries will be made in Wilson's account to show how settlement of the £200 due has been made. First, an entry for £194 with a corresponding debit entry in the bank account for the amount of the cheque. Second, an entry for £6 with a corresponding debit entry for the discount allowed. The accounts will then look like this:

Dr		B. Wilson			Cr
		£			£
18 May	Sales	200	4 June	Bank	194
			4 June	Discount allowed	6

Discount allowed		
4 June	B. Wilson	6

Bank		
4 June	B. Wilson	194

Bad debts

This is the expense incurred when debtors fail to pay their debts. In the balance sheet, debtors appear as an asset because it is assumed that anyone to whom credit has been allowed will pay what they owe. Once it is known that a debt is never going to be collected this fact must be shown in the accounts. If it were not then the accounts would not be giving a fair picture of the assets of the business. For example, Ron Evans, who for a short and unsuccessful time was a retailer, owes a wholesaler £180. The wholesaler has been unable to collect his money and has just heard that there is no likelihood that he ever will. He must remove the asset by making a credit entry in the debtor's account. The corresponding debit entry will be in an account termed 'bad debts'. The accounts will look like this:

Dr		Ron Evans			Cr
		£			£
6 Jan.	Sales	180	10 Oct.	Bad debts	180

	Bad debts	
10 Oct.	R. Evans	180

In effect an asset has been converted into an expense. Naturally any firm allowing credit to another takes all reasonable precautions to make certain that this kind of thing does not happen too often. It is accepted, however, that 'writing off' a bad debt, as this process is called, is an occasional and inevitable part of allowing credit to others.

Activity

Put yourself in the position of a wholesaler who has just received a request from a retailer that he should be allowed to make use of the monthly credit terms allowed to other retailers. What steps would you take to minimise the possibility of bad debts?

RESPONSE

There are a number of possibilities. References could be requested from other firms with which the retailer has been dealing. You might give monthly credit only when he has proved to be a reliable payer on a weekly basis. Perhaps a maximum credit limit could be set for a trial period to reduce the risk of large debts not being paid.

Whatever you do, the risk of non-payment by some debtors always exists. It is important, therefore, to act quickly when a slow or bad payer is identified and to try to prevent the loss involved being too great. This might involve correspondence from yourself or even a solicitor. In the case of larger debts you will have to decide whether legal action, which can sometimes be very costly, is worthwhile. If all this fails the value of the asset, debtor, must be reduced in the manner described.

Depreciation

This is the expense incurred when one of the fixed assets owned by a business falls in value. Just as 'debtors' cannot be allowed to include any amounts which it is known will not be collected, so it would be wrong to allow an asset, such as motor vehicles, equipment, machinery or furniture and fittings, to be valued at a figure greater than its true worth.

By now you should have grasped what kind of entry in an asset account is needed to reduce the value of that asset: a credit entry. Refer back to page 45 if you thought otherwise. The corresponding debit entry will be in an account named 'depreciation on . . .' (the name of the fixed asset involved).

For example, B. Wilson purchased a delivery van on 27 April for £1,500. By 31 December of that year it was worth only £1,100. Its value had fallen or depreciated by £400. This would be shown in the accounts like this:

Dr		Delivery vehicle			Cr
		£			£
27 April	Bank	1,500	31 Dec.	Depreciation	400

Depreciation on delivery vehicle		
31 Dec. Delivery vehicle	400	

Discount allowed, bad debts and depreciation are all expenses commonly incurred in running a business. The difference between them and other expenses like rent, rates and insurance is that, instead of a direct money payment being made, an asset other than bank or cash is reduced in value.

> ### Self-check
>
> Which asset is reduced in value under the following circumstances?
>
> **a** Rent is paid by cheque.
> **b** A customer is allowed 3% discount for prompt payment.
> **c** Wages are paid in cash.
> **d** A customer unable to pay an amount owed.
> **e** It is discovered that machinery purchased for £1,000 is now worth £800.

ANSWER

a Bank, **b** debtor, **c** cash, **d** debtor, **e** machinery.

Incomes

While all businesses will have to pay for a variety of expenses to enable them to operate, some will also receive income for the services they provide for others. For many businesses the major receipt of money will come from sales of their stock, an item dealt with at the beginning of this chapter. Here we are concerned with those receipts of money which come from sources other than sales of stock. For example, a business may own property which it does not need for its own use but which it does not wish to sell. Renting this property to another firm will enable it to gain useful income. Similarly one firm may provide a service for another and charge commission. Care is needed in the accounts to distinguish such receipts from payments. It is usual to label an account for income received from letting out property 'rent received account' to avoid confusion with the rent account which is for the expense involved when another's property is used by the firm itself. Similarly, commission account will be for the expense, and commission received account for the income.

The entries to be made in accounts recording incomes will be opposite to those demonstrated for expenses. When the money is received an asset account such as bank is increased by a debit entry. At the same time a compensating credit entry is made in the income account.

Self-check

A retailer lets the flat above his shop for £80 a month. This is paid in cash on the first of each month. Show the relevant entries for March in the retailer's accounts.

ANSWER

Dr		Cash			Cr
		£			£
1 March	Rent received	80			

		Rent received			
			1 March	Cash	80

Discount received

An income which many businesses enjoy comes from settling the amounts due to their suppliers promptly. This is known as discount received. It takes the form of a reduction in the amount that has to be paid rather than an actual physical receipt of money. Thus the debit entry corresponding to the credit entry in the discount received account will be in the creditor's account, showing the reduction of a liability. For example, a retailer purchases goods for £400 from Western Suppliers on 3 July. A discount of 2% is offered for settlement received by 31 July so the retailer pays by cheque on 30 July. Relevant entries in the accounts of the retailer follow.

Dr			Western Suppliers		Cr
		£			£
30 July	Bank	392	3 July Purchases		400
30 July	Discount received	8			

Bank

			30 July	Western Suppliers	392

Discount received

			30 July	Western Suppliers	8

It is important to make the two debit entries in the account for Western Suppliers simultaneously. Otherwise it might seem that £8 was still owing at the end of the month and a payment might be made.

It is possible to summarise all the reasons for making a debit or credit entry in the form of a ledger account.

Reasons for making an entry in its own account	
Debit	*Credit*
1 An opening asset value	1 Opening value of a source of finance
2 Increasing asset value	2 Increase of a source of finance
3 An expense	3 An income
4 Increase in an expense	4 Increase in an income
5 Reduction of a source of finance	5 Reduction of an asset
6 Reduction of an income	6 Reduction of an expense

You can use this as a quick means of reference when in doubt about whether a credit or debit entry is needed. Remember, sources of finance include capital and liabilities. Try it now if you need to.

Self-check

Complete the table below to show the entries needed to record the transactions.

Transaction	Account to be debited	Account to be credited
a Payment of rates by cheque.		
b Purchase of goods for resale on credit from Asta Suppliers.		
c Purchase of office desk for cash.		
d Commission received by cheque for services rendered.		
e Deducted discount for prompt settlement of amount owing to Asta Suppliers.		
f Discovery of error resulting in repayment by cheque of part of the commission received.		

ANSWER

a Dr rates, cr bank.
b Dr purchases, cr Asta Suppliers.
c Dr office furniture or similar, cr cash.
d Dr bank, cr commission rec.
e Dr Asta Suppliers, cr discount rec.
f Dr commission received, cr bank.

If you managed to reason out this self-check, you should be able to tackle the following exercise which involves much of the work encountered so far.

Exercise

Helen Berry started a retail business on 1 March 1982 with £3,000 in the bank, furniture and fittings worth £3,000 and premises valued at £15,000. She had borrowed £2,000 from Busifinance Ltd for six months.

Draft a balance sheet and open ledger accounts for all the items included. Enter the following transactions in the ledger, opening new accounts where necessary.

2 March	Purchased on credit £1,000 stock from Northern Foods and £500 stock from AKJ.
3 March	Sales for cash £50.
4 March	Sales for cash £100.
5 March	Paid £80 cash into bank.
6 March	Returned £100 of goods to AKJ.
7 March	Paid amount owing to Northern Foods by cheque less 2% discount.
8 March	Sold goods for £100 to N. Timms on credit.
9 March	Paid insurance £25 by cheque.
10 March	Received £20 cash for letting the flat above the shop.

Note that you have to calculate the owner's capital yourself. If you have any difficulty, compare the following solution with your own. It is advisable to check each transaction one at a time in date order.

ANSWER

Balance sheet of Helen Berry as at 1 March 1982

	£		£	£
Owner's capital	19,000	*Fixed assets*		
		Premises	15,000	
		Furniture and fittings	3,000	
				18,000
Current liabilities		*Current assets*		
Busifinance Ltd	2,000	Bank		3,000
	21,000			21,000

Dr		Premises			Cr
		£			£
1 March	Balance	15,000			

		Furniture and fittings			
1 March	Balance	3,000			

		Bank			
1 March	Balance	3,000	7 March	Northern Foods	980
5 March	Cash	80	9 March	Insurance	25

		Capital			
			1 March	Balance	19,000

		Busifinance			
			1 March	Balance	2,000

		Purchases			
2 March	Northern Foods	1,000			
2 March	AKJ	500			

		Northern Foods			
7 March	Bank	980	2 March	Purchases	1,000
7 March	Disct recd	20			

Dr		AKJ			Cr
		£			£
6 March	Purchases returns	100	2 March	Purchases	500

		Sales		
			3 March	Cash	50
			4 March	Cash	100
			8 March	N. Timms	100

		Cash			
3 March	Sales	50	5 March	Bank	80
4 March	Sales	100			
10 March	Rent received	20			

		Purchases returns		
			6 March	AKJ	100

		Discount received		
			7 March	Northern Foods	20

		N. Timms		
8 March	Sales	100		

		Insurance		
9 March	Bank	25		

		Rent received		
			10 March	Cash	20

6 | The trial balance

The last two chapters concerned the rules of double-entry book-keeping and the application of these rules to a variety of transactions. In this chapter we are going to look at a simple way of making a preliminary check on the accuracy of the entries made in the ledger. We will do this by balancing the accounts and then drafting a trial balance. I will start, however, by demonstrating how the folio column in the ledger can be used to provide a reference system for all the double entries. Such a system helps to speed up the process of checking that all the double entries have been completed correctly.

The folio column in the ledger is the only one we have not used so far. Remind yourself of its position by looking back at the diagram in Chapter 4, page 40. You will remember that a folio is a page or leaf of a book and that all pages in the ledger will be numbered. We can use these numbers to provide us with our reference system. An example should make this clear. This a/c appears in the ledger of a wholesaler.

Dr			£ p		Tom Paxton	44	Cr £ p
1 Aug.	Sales	26	100.00	2 Aug.	Return in	32	25.00
4 Aug.	Sales	26	8.00	5 Aug.	Bank	12	70.00
				5 Aug.	Discount allowed	38	5.00

Tom's account is on page 44 of the ledger (or on a ledger card numbered 44). The entry in the folio column for each transaction tells us on which page of the ledger the other entry can be found. From this you can deduce that the account for sales is on page 26, returns inward on page 32, bank on page 12 and discount allowed on page 38. Looking for a numbered page or card is much quicker than looking for the name of an account when you are checking to make certain that all entries have been completed correctly.

Self-check

Show the entries in the sales account which relate to the transaction of 1 and 4 August. You should head the sales account with the page number on which it is to be found and complete the folio column.

ANSWER

Dr		Sales account		26	Cr
					£ p
	1 Aug.	Tom Paxton	44	100.00	
	4 Aug.	Tom Paxton	44	8.00	

Did you show in your sales account that the account for Tom Paxton will be found on page 44 and that the sales account is on page 26? If so, good. If not, look again at the account of Tom Paxton.

This system is fairly simple to understand but it does require care when making the entries. To avoid having too much detail in the accounts I do not intend to keep a reference system for all the exercises. It is worthwhile, however, checking your understanding of this use of the folio column by completing the following.

Exercise

Look again at the solution to the last exercise in Chapter 4, page 51. Number each account from premises (1) to JLK (9). These will represent the page numbers on which these accounts can be found. Then complete the folio column correctly for each entry. You will not have a reference for those entries described as 'balance'. Soon we will find a use for the folio column in dealing with such entries.

RESPONSE

Common sense will probably have been your guide in this activity. You will 'feel' that you have done it correctly. As a check I will reproduce the furniture and fittings account as it should look after you have inserted the references. If you did this correctly the chances are that the others will also be right.

Dr			Furniture and fittings account		2	Cr
		£				£
1 July	Balance	2,000	4 July	S. Moore	8	50
2 July	Bank	4	300	4 July	Cash	5	50
5 July	Bank loan	7	500				

Balancing accounts

Let's turn now to checking the accuracy of transactions made in the ledger. To do this, you must learn the technique of balancing the ledger accounts. The balance of an account is the difference between the two sides. This is the most significant figure in the account because it tells us the value of the asset, liability, expense or income of which the account is a record. When the debit side is greater it is termed a debit balance. Conversely, credit balance indicates the difference when that side of the account is greater.

> ### Self-check
>
> Look back at my solution in Chapter 5, page 73. Calculate the balance in each account and state what kind of balance it is.

ANSWER

Premises £15,000 dr balance; furniture and fittings £3,000 dr balance; bank £2,075 dr balance; capital £19,000 cr balance; Busifinance £2,000 cr balance; purchases £1,500 dr balance; AKJ £400 cr balance; sales £250 cr balance; cash £90 dr balance; purchases returns £100 cr balance; discount recd. £20 cr balance; N. Timms £100 dr balance; insurance £25 dr balance; rent received £20 cr balance.

Provided you understood that the balance is the difference between the two sides of an account and that it is described by debit when that side is greater and credit when that side is greater, this should not have caused you any problems. In many of the accounts there was only one entry on one side. In some of these, e.g. premises and capital, that one entry was described as balance in the details column. This was because that opening entry had come directly from the list of balances in the balance sheet.

We can now proceed to the method used to show what the balance is at a particular time. This is known as balancing the accounts. Let's assume that Helen Berry's accounts which we used in the last self-check are to be balanced on 10 March. This is what her bank account will look like after it has been balanced:

Dr		£		Bank account	Cr £
1 March	Balance	3,000	7 March	Northern Foods	980
5 March	Cash	80	9 March	Insurance	25
			10 March	Balance c/d	2,075
		3,080			3,080
11 March	Balance b/d	2,075			

This, in stages, is how it is done:

1 Find the difference between the two sides.
2 Place this figure on the side of the account that is smaller. It is described as balance c/d which means that the balance is to be carried down. The date is that on which the account is being balanced.
3 Total the two sides, drawing the lines carefully so that the two totals are level with each other. As the difference between the two sides has been added to the smaller side both sides will now be equal.
4 Enter the balance on to the side to which it really belongs, describing it as the balance b/d which means that the balance has been brought down. It is dated one day after that of the balance carried down figure. The folio column is used for c/d and b/d.

In the above account we can now tell at a glance that, when business starts on 11 March, Helen Berry has £2,075 in her asset bank account. The significance of dating the balance to be carried down one day earlier than the balance which has been brought down is that the account is shown as being temporarily closed at the end of business on one day and then reopened, with the same amount, when business begins next day.

Self-check

Balance Helen's cash account on page 74 for 10 March. Take care to follow the stages I have outlined.

ANSWER

Dr			Cash account			Cr
			£			£
3 March	Sales		50	5 March	Bank	80
4 March	Sales		100	10 March	Balance c/d	90
10 March	Rent received		20			
			170			170
11 March	Balance b/d		90			

Stage 1 The difference between the two sides is £90.
Stage 2 This is placed on the smaller side with the description balance carried down.
Stage 3 Totals of each side are then shown equal and level.
Stage 4 The balance is brought down to the side to which it belongs for the start of business next day.

Where there is only one entry in an account, that is the balance or difference between the two sides. It perhaps seems unnecessary to go through the process of balancing such an account. However this is still done by some people and it does serve as a means of showing that all the accounts have been looked at and brought up to date at the same time. For example, it is not likely that the premises account will contain many new entries from one year to the next. Suppose Helen Berry decides to balance it at the end of her current financial year which will be on 28 February 1983. This is how it will look:

Dr		Premises account			Cr
1982		£	*1983*		£
1 March	Balance	15,000	28 February	Balance c/d	15,000
1983					
1 March	Balance b/d	15,000			

The procedure is the same as above except that there is no need to total the two sides. When the balance to be carried down is inserted on the smaller, credit, side both sides are immediately equal. Underlining the two figures is enough to show they are the totals.

Self-check

Balance the account of N. Timms on 31 March 1982.

ANSWER

Dr		N. Timms account			Cr
		£			£
8 March	Sales	100	31 March	Balance c/d	100
1 April	Balance b/d	100			

If you feel you need the practice you could balance the remainder of Helen's accounts, choosing any date you wish. Remember, however, the balance brought down will be dated the day after the balance carried down.

When should accounts be balanced? There is no hard and fast rule. Occasions when it is often done include: the need for a new page of an account when the existing page is full and at the end of a firm's financial year. There is in fact nothing to prevent an account being balanced at any time when it is felt that the information it reveals will be useful. One such occasion might be when a check is to be made on the accuracy of entries made in the ledger accounts. It is to this that we will now turn.

A brief summary of what has been learnt so far about double entry book-keeping will help to show how the balances in the accounts can be used as a means of checking the accuracy of the entries within. The following diagram is virtually self-explanatory.

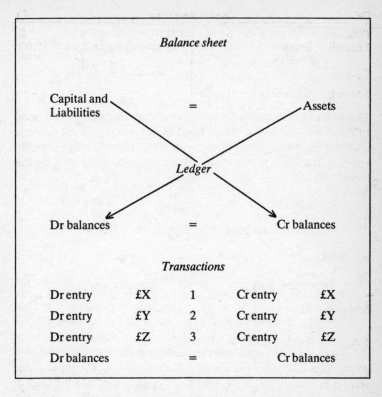

We begin with the balance sheet which reflected the book-keeping equation, i.e. *sources of finance (capital* and *liabilities)* must equal the *assets.* In the ledger each asset was shown as a debit balance in its own account and each source of finance as a credit balance. Therefore the debit balances will equal the credit balances. When transactions are entered in the ledger additional accounts may be opened but whatever the transaction it will involve a debit entry of the same amount as the corresponding credit entry. Therefore after any number of transactions the total value of the debit balances *should* still equal the total value of the credit balances.

Checking that the debit balances do in fact equal the credit balances is done by making a list of all the balances. This is known as a trial balance and usually takes the following form.

Trial balance of Helen Berry as at 10 March 1982

Accounts	Dr balances £	Cr balances £
Premises	15,000	
Furniture and fittings	3,000	
Bank	2,075	
Capital		19,000
Busifinance		2,000
Purchases	1,500	
Northern Foods	—	—
AKJ		400
Sales		250
Cash	90	
Purchases returns		100
Discount received		20
N. Timms	100	
Insurance	25	
Rent received		20
	21,790	21,790

The figures contained in the above trial balance have been obtained from the accounts of Helen Berry in Chapter 5, page 73. Note that, as there is no balance at present in the Northern Foods account, it is not essential to show that account in the trial balance. The fact that the total debit balances equals the total of the credit balances is sufficient evidence to prove that the transactions have been entered correctly in the ledger. To give you practice in entering transactions and checking their accuracy by drafting a trial balance, work through the following exercise.

Exercise

Mike Bishop opened his petrol service station on 1 May 1982. He had £1,000 in the bank, £200 in cash, £8,000 worth of stock and machinery and equipment worth £12,000. He had borrowed £4,000 from Petrofinance Ltd for nine months and provided the rest of the finance himself.

1 Draft a balance sheet to show Mike's position on 1 May 1982, taking care to calculate the figure for owner's capital.

2 Open a ledger account for each item and enter the opening balances.

3 Enter the following transactions in the ledger, opening new accounts where necessary. Then extract a trial balance on 7 May to check the accuracy of your entries.

2 May Cash sales £600.

3 May Cash sales £550; purchases £1,200 on credit from PB Ltd.

4 May Cash sales £720; paid £1,500 cash into bank.

5 May Cash sales £680; paid rent £160 by cheque.

6 May Cash sales £540; purchases £200 on credit from Greas-oils Ltd.

7 May Paid amount owing to PB Ltd, less 3% discount by cheque.

ANSWERS

Balance sheet of Mike Bishop as at 1 May 1982

	£		£	£
Sources of finance		*Fixed assets*		
Owner's capital	17,200	Equipment and machinery		12,000
Current liabilities		*Current assets*		
Petrofinance Ltd	4,000	Stock	8,000	
		Bank	1,000	
		Cash	200	
				9,200
	21,200			21,200

Dr		Equipment and machinery			Cr
1982		£			£
1 May	Balance	12,000			

Dr		Stock			Cr
		£			£
1 May	Balance	8,000			

		Bank			
1 May	Balance	1,000	5 May	Rent	160
4 May	Cash	1,500	7 May	PB Ltd	1,164
			7 May	Balance c/d	1,176
		2,500			2,500
8 May	Balance b/d	1,176			

		Cash			
1 May	Balance	200	4 May	Bank	1,500
2 May	Sales	600	7 May	Balance c/d	1,790
3 May	Sales	550			
4 May	Sales	720			
5 May	Sales	680			
6 May	Sales	540			
		3,290			3,290
7 May	Balance b/d	1,790			

		Capital			
			1982		
			1 May	Balance	17,200

		Petrofinance Ltd			
			1 May	Balance	4,000

		Sales			
7 May	Balance c/d	3,090	2 May	Cash	600
			3 May	Cash	550
			4 May	Cash	720
			5 May	Cash	680
			6 May	Cash	540
		3,090			3,090
			8 May	Balance b/d	3,090

Dr			Purchases		Cr
3 May	PB Ltd	1,200	7 May	Balance c/d	1,400
6 May	Greasoils	200			
		1,400			1,400
8 May	Balance b/d	1,400			

			PB Ltd		
7 May	Bank	1,164	3 May	Purchases	1,200
7 May	Discount recd	36			

			Rent		
5 May	Bank	160			

			Greasoils Ltd		
			6 May	Purchases	200

			Discount received		
			7 May	PB Ltd	36

Trial balance of Mike Bishop as at 7 May 1982

	Dr balances £	Cr balances £
Equipment and machinery	12,000	
Stock	8,000	
Bank	1,176	
Cash	1,790	
Capital		17,200
Petrofinance Ltd		4,000
Sales		3,090
Purchases	1,400	
Rent	160	
Greasoils		200
Discount recd		36
	24,526	24,526

I have balanced only those accounts which contain more than one entry. In the others the sole entry stands out clearly and this is the balance of that account.

Did your trial balance add up to the same totals as mine? If so you have probably completed the exercise correctly. If not, check through your solution stage by stage:

1 Make certain that you calculated the owner's capital correctly and that the balance sheet balanced with the same totals as mine.

2 Check that the assets and sources of finance were entered on the correct side of their accounts. The opening debit balances (assets) should, of course, equal the total credit balances (capital and liabilities).

3 Go through each transaction following the rules on page 70. Make sure that for each debit entry there is a corresponding credit entry of the same value.

4 Check that you have calculated the balances on each account accurately, paying particular attention to those accounts with most entries. Remember the balance of an account is the difference between the two sides. It is described as a debit balance when the total value of debit entries is greater than the credits. If the credit side is greater than the debit the difference is a credit balance.

5 Make certain that you have put the balances in the right column of the trial balance.

Dealing with errors
Practice helps to eliminate mistakes and aids in finding them more quickly when they do occur. Sometimes, though, finding why the trial balance does not agree proves to be very difficult, especially in a large firm where hundreds of transactions are being recorded in a single day. There may simply not be enough time available to look for the errors. What can be done? One way round this problem is to invent an account and debit or credit it with the amount needed to make the trial balance agree. This account is called a suspense account. When the error is discovered the suspense account can be closed.

For example, on 30 April the debit balances in our firm's trial balance total £100 more than the credit balances and a suspense account is opened.

Dr		Suspense account		Cr
				£
	30 April	Difference		
		in books		100

If this credit balance is added to the trial balance the debits will now equal the credits. They have been made to be equal.

Suppose that on 27 May Mr Chandler writes to complain that the statement we have sent him shows that he owes £450 when in fact he owes £350 because he paid £100 by cheque on 28 April. When this is checked we discover that a debit entry has been made in our bank account to record the money received but no credit entry has been made in Mr Chandler's account to reduce the amount he owes. We can put matters right by debiting the suspense account and crediting the account of Mr Chandler. We should also apologise to him of course! The accounts will then look like this:

Dr		Suspense account		Cr
	£			£
27 May Chandler	100	30 April	Difference	
			in books	100

M. Chandler

		£			£
1 May	Balance	450	27 May Suspense account		100

The suspense account is closed until it is needed again and Mr Chandler's account is reduced by £100 to a debit balance of £350. Provided no other errors have been made in the meantime a trial balance extracted now would agree.

Self-check

Imagine your trial balance of 30 June shows that the credit balances are £50 greater than the debits. £50 discount received for promptly settling an amount owing to K. Bryant has been entered on the credit side of the discount received account but has not been debited to Bryant's account.

First open a suspense account to record the difference in the books on 30 June. Then show the double entries which would be made to correct the error.

ANSWER

Dr			Suspense account		Cr
		£			£
30 June	Difference in books	50	12 July K. Bryant		50

	K. Bryant		
12 July	Suspense account	50	

Although useful as a means of checking the accuracy of transactions recorded in the ledger, the trial balance is not foolproof. There are some errors which it will not reveal. These are often grouped into five types:

Review

1 Study the account of B. John, which has been extracted
from the ledger of G. Edwards, and answer the questions
which follow it.

B. John					39
1981		£	1981		£
1 May	Balance b/d	150	8 May	Bank	6 140
17 May	Sales 21	250	8 May	Discount allowed 12	10
27 May	Sales 21	130			

a Define the term 'balance' and explain what it means
on 1 May in the above account.
b Explain the two entries of 8 May. To what do '6' and
'12' refer?
c Balance the account correctly on 31 May.

2 What is a trial balance and why is it used?
3 An inexperienced book-keeper has drafted the following
trial balance. He has made some basic errors which you
should be able to correct. The totals of the trial balance
will then agree.

Trial balance of John Williams as at 30 April 1981

	£ dr	£ cr
Capital		20,000
Premises	12,000	
Equipment	4,000	
Debtors		2,000
Creditors	1,000	
Stock	5,000	
Rent and rates	1,000	
Insurance	400	
Wages		8,600
Sales	40,000	
Purchases		25,000
Cash in bank	3,000	
	66,400	55,600

    4 Name the types of error which will not be revealed by drafting a trial balance.

    5 A cheque for £60 received from M. Smith has been incorrectly credited to the account of M. J. K. Smith. Show the entries needed to correct the error.

ANSWERS

1 a The balance is the difference between the two sides of an account. The debit balance of 1 May indicates that B. John is a debtor to Edwards for £150.

  b On 8 May, John settled the amount owing from last month. He paid £140 by cheque and was allowed £10 discount for prompt payment. The bank account will be found on page 6 of the ledger and the account for discount allowed on page 12.

  c

Dr			B. John			39	Cr
1981		£	1981				£
1 May	Balance b/d	150	8 May	Bank	6	140
17 May	Sales	21	250	8 May	Discount allowed	12	10
27 May	Sales	21	130	31 May	Balance c/d		380
		530					530
1 June	Balance b/d	380					

2 A trial balance is a list of all the balances in the ledger accounts at a particular time. It is used to check on the accuracy of the entries. If correct, the total value of the debit balances should equal the total value of credit balances.

3 You should have noticed that the balances for debtors, creditors, wages, sales and purchases were placed in the wrong column of the trial balance. If you change them around, the totals will agree at £61,000.

4 Errors of omission, errors of commission. errors of principle, compensating errors and original errors.

5

Dr	M. J. K. Smith		Cr
	£		£
M. Smith	60		

	M. Smith	
	M. J. K. Smith	60

The debit entry in M. J. K. Smith's account removes the mistake and the credit entry in M. Smith's account corrects it.

7 | The cash book

In this chapter we will see how the contents of a ledger can be subdivided into a number of sections. We will then deal in some detail with one of these subdivisions – the cash book.

So far, we have been thinking of the ledger as one book containing all the accounts. This has one obvious disadvantage. Only one person may use it at any one time. This might not matter in a small business where there are only a few transactions each day. In a larger business, however, where there may be many different transactions, and more than one accounts clerk employed, real difficulties will be encountered. The idea of subdividing the ledger to enable the work of recording transactions to be shared and carried out more efficiently appealed to many businesses. The diagram below summarises the main ways in which this was done.

Divisions of the ledger

S t a g e	General ledger			
1	General ledger			Cash book
2	General ledger	Debtors' ledger	Creditors' ledger	Cash book
3	General ledger	Private ledger	Debtors' ledger	Creditors' ledger	Cash book

The first stage is to take out the two accounts which are most used – the cash account and bank account – and place them in a separate book, which becomes known as the cash book. All other accounts remain in the general ledger. The second stage involves extracting from the general ledger the debtors and creditors accounts. These are then kept in their own separate books. Note that the terms 'purchases ledger' and 'bought ledger' are sometimes used instead of creditors' ledger, and 'sales ledger' instead of debtors' ledger. Goods purchased on credit are bought from creditors. Sales on credit are made to debtors. Whichever terms you choose, it is best to use them consistently.

The names of the new divisions of the ledger are a good indication of the accounts contained within them. This is true also when the third stage is reached and some accounts are withdrawn and placed in the private ledger. Clearly such a book will contain any accounts which the owner wishes to keep private. The capital account is one example, and drawings account (which we will meet later) is another. Again all other accounts not withdrawn into a separate book remain in the general ledger.

It should not be thought that these stages have to occur in the order I have given. Some owners might have decided to extract their private accounts from the prying eyes of their clerk before even considering the practical advantages to be gained by putting the cash and bank accounts together in the cash book. Nor should it be thought that all businesses which open a debtors' ledger will automatically open a creditors' ledger. A business with a large number of customers, to whom it sells on credit, will probably find it advantageous to have a separate ledger to contain them. If, however, it purchases stock from only a few suppliers it might not be worth taking these accounts out of the general ledger. Further, there is nothing to prevent a business subdividing its accounts to an even greater extent than the diagram suggests. One common occurrence, for example, is for businesses with large numbers of debtors' accounts to have them entered on cards and kept in a filing system. These debtors might be filed alphabetically in a drawer with A–D kept separate from E–H, etc. The diagram does, however, give a general summary of how a ledger might be subdivided.

Self-check

EBA Ltd has a cash book, debtors' ledger and a general
ledger. In which of these would you find the following
accounts? **a** T. Smith, a customer, **b** wages account, **c** bank
account, **d** A. Lindsay, a supplier.

ANSWER

a Debtors' ledger, **b** general ledger, **c** cash book, **d** general
ledger. This should not have caused you too much trouble.
Remember that, if there is no division of the ledger for a
particular sort of account, it remains in the general ledger. If
EBA had kept a creditors' ledger, Lindsay's account would have
been in it. As they didn't the account will appear with numerous
different accounts, including the wages account, in the general
ledger.

It is also possible to classify ledger accounts into personal and
impersonal accounts. The former comprises the accounts of
people and other firms with which a business deals and the latter
all other accounts. The impersonal accounts can be further
subdivided into real accounts and nominal accounts. Real
accounts are those in which a record is kept of the assets of a
business. They are real in the sense that it is possible to touch
them – for example, buildings, furniture, cash. Nominal
accounts contain the records of income and expenses. Rent,
rates and insurance are common examples of expenses while
discount received and commission received are examples of
incomes which we met earlier. Nominal means 'in name only'.
The rent account may have a balance of £1,000 but the money
will not really be there. Similarly, the commission received
account may show that £200 was received last month but the
money may now be spent. The following diagram summarises
this classification.

Types of account

Personal (debtors and creditors)	Impersonal (all other accounts)	
Personal (debtors and creditors)	Real accounts (assets)	Nominal accounts (incomes and expenses)

Self-check

Classify the following accounts as real, nominal or personal. **a** Peter Finch, supplier, **b** wages, **c** stock, **d** Robin Withe, customer, **e** machinery, **f** bank, **g** rent received, **h** capital.

ANSWER

c, **e** and **f** are real accounts because they are assets. **b** and **g** are nominal accounts, wages being an expense and rent received an income. **a**, **d** and **h** are personal accounts. You may have encountered two classification problems here. First, it could be argued that as a debtor is an asset the account for Robin Withe might be classified as real rather than personal. The personal aspect takes priority, however, in this case, as the division between personal and impersonal accounts comes before the further subdivision of impersonal accounts into real and nominal. This should be clear if you look again at the diagram.

Second, how should capital be classified? It is regarded as a special kind of personal account recording the relationship of the business with a person – the owner. The owner's capital can be regarded as the sum owing to him by the business.

Placing accounts in separate sections in the ledger causes no major book-keeping problems, though some thought must be given to adapting the reference system used. The abbreviations GL, DL, and CL and CB normally appear alongside the title of the account to show in which section of the ledger it is positioned. They also prefix the page number of the double entry which is recorded in the folio column.

Self-check

To what do the letters GL, DL, CL and CB refer?

ANSWER

You should have had little difficulty in recognising these as short for general ledger, debtors' ledger, creditors' ledger and cash book.

The two-column cash book
In the cash book it is usual not just to keep a separate account for cash and bank records but also to combine the accounts together to form one unit. The rest of this chapter will be devoted to different ways of using the cash book. The opposite page shows an example of what is known as a two-column cash book.

From our earlier work, when the cash and bank accounts were kept separately in the ledger, you should have recalled that the debit entries record money received which increases the assets, cash or bank. Credit entries are used to record payments of money which decrease the assets, cash or bank. Although the accounts for cash and bank have been combined together they are still in reality separate. The debit entries for cash must be kept apart from the debit entries for bank and the credit entries must also be kept apart. It is very important, therefore, to label the columns clearly. By convention, the cash column appears to the left of the bank column.

Cash book

Dr						Cr				
Date	Details	F	Cash	Bank		Date	Details	F	Cash	Bank
1 Feb.	Balances	b/d	100.20	700.60		2 Feb.	Postage	GL 4	12.15	
3 Feb.	Sales	GL 6	220.60			3 Feb.	N. Keegan	CL 9		150.00
4 Feb.	C. Winston	DL 41		320.50		4 Feb.	Purchases	GL 12		260.00
5 Feb.	N. Jones	DL 20		110.90		6 Feb.	Rates	GL 15		79.00
8 Feb.	Sales	GL 6	600.20			7 Feb.	Wages	GL 19	60.00	
9 Feb.	Cash	c		750.00		9 Feb.	Bank	c	750.00	
11 Feb.	R. Starr	DL 31		140.30		10 Feb.	R. Willis	CL10	60.00	
13 Feb.	Bank	c	150.00			12 Feb.	Insurance	GL 6	20.00	
						13 Feb.	Cash	c		150.00
						14 Feb.	Balances	c/d	168.85	1,383.30
			1,071.00	2,022.30					1,071.00	2,022.30
15 Feb.	Balances	b/d	168.85	1,383.30						

You should be able to explain each of the entries in the cash book. To make certain, attempt the following.

Self-check

Explain in your own words the transactions dated 2 Feb., 5 Feb., 6 Feb., 8 Feb., 9 Feb. and 13 Feb.

ANSWER

2 Feb. Paid postage £12.15 cash. 5 Feb. Received cheque from N. Jones for £110.90. 6 Feb. Paid rates by cheque £79.00. 8 Feb. Cash sales £600.20. Provided you remembered that a debit entry increases an asset while a credit entry reduces it, these should not have caused you any problems. The final two transactions are a little more complicated, however, because the entries for both transactions are in the same book: 9 Feb. £750 cash was paid into the bank.

It is worth expanding on this explanation because it often causes confusion. The debit entry in the bank column shows that the money in the bank has increased by £750. The description 'cash' explains how. We know that the description given should be the name of the other account affected. The credit entry is to be found therefore in the cash column. As a credit entry in an asset account shows a reduction in the value of the asset, the cash has been reduced by £750. The description for the credit entry in the cash column is 'bank', the name of the other account affected.

Now look at the folio columns for the two entries of 9 Feb. The letter 'c' is short for *contra*, a Latin term for opposite or against. It is used here to indicate that the double entry is on the same page of the same book.

13 Feb. – £150 was withdrawn from the bank for use as cash. Note that this is the reverse of the transaction of 9 Feb. The debit entry in the cash column shows this asset increasing and the credit entry in the bank column shows that asset decreasing. A 'c' for *contra* again appears in the folio columns and each description gives the name of the other column affected. If you ever have an entry in the bank column described as 'bank' or in the cash column described as 'cash' you will know immediately that an error has been made.

Exercise

Rewrite the cash and bank accounts on page 84 as they would appear in a two-column cash book. It is possible to buy a variety of types of cash books or loose-leaf paper from good stationers but it is not difficult to rule your own. You need not complete the folio column unless there is a *contra* entry.

ANSWER

Cash book

		Cash	Bank				Cash	Bank
1 May Balances	b/d	200	1,000	4 May	Bank	c	1,500	
2 May Sales		600		5 May	Rent			160
3 May Sales		550		7 May	PB Ltd			1,164
4 May Sales		720		7 May	Balances	c/d	1,790	1,176
4 May Cash	c		1,500					
5 May Sales		680						
6 May Sales		540						
		3,290	2,500				3,290	2,500
8 May Balances	b/d	1,790	1,176					

Note the diagonal line on the credit side between the last entry and the totals. This is done by some book-keepers to prevent an entry being made in an account in the wrong place after it has been balanced.

The three-column cash book

Combining the cash and bank accounts together in one book, so that current transactions in cash and by cheque are recorded together, makes for far greater efficiency. This can be taken a step further. In many businesses payments to suppliers are timed to enable the business to receive a discount. At the same time money will be received from customers who will have deducted discount allowed in return for prompt settlement. There are thus going to be many entries for discount allowed associated with the money received from customers and many entries for discount received associated with money paid to suppliers. A simple way of recording these discounts in the cash book at the same time as the money is recorded will further increase efficiency. This can be done by extending the cash book into a three-column cash book. See the example on page 103.

The only additions to the two-column cash book we looked at earlier are the columns for discount allowed to customers on the debit side and the column for discount received from suppliers on the credit side. We will concentrate here on these additions and the transactions involved.

On 3 May the supplier B. Thomas was paid £206.29 by cheque. The credit entry in the bank column shows this. We also see that £4.21 discount has been received for paying promptly. This is deducted when payment is made because it will be known then whether the discount can be claimed. This is preferable to paying the full amount due and then receiving a rebate later. The debit entries relating to both the cheque and the discount received will be in the account of B. Thomas.

Self-check

Look at the credit entry dated 4 May.
1 How much would have had to be paid to J. Rees if the payment had not been made in the time specified?
2 Calculate the percentage discount being received for prompt payment.

ANSWERS

1 £100. The discount received of £2 could not have been claimed and the cheque paid would have had to cover this amount as well as the £98 which was paid.
2

$$\frac{\text{discount}}{\text{total amount due}} \times \frac{100}{1} = \frac{2}{100} \times \frac{100}{1} = 2\%.$$

There are three other transactions involving discount received on the credit side of the cash book and they are similar to the ones we have considered. Look now at the balancing of the accounts on 14 May. Cash and bank balances are obtained and

Cash book

Dr Date	Details	Fol.	Discount allowed	Cash	Bank	Cr Date	Details	Fol.	Discount received	Cash	Bank
1 May	Balances	b/d		115.20	760.50	2 May	Wages			80.00	
2 May	Sales			120.80		3 May	B. Thomas		4.21		206.29
3 May	Sales			109.55		4 May	J. Rees		2.00		98.00
4 May	R. Evans		12.00		388.00	5 May	W. Jones		3.01		147.49
5 May	Sales			96.47		6 May	B. Robson			88.47	
6 May	Sales			80.21		7 May	Bank	c		190.00	
7 May	Cash	c			190.00	7 May	Rent				45.00
8 May	J. Morris		1.77		86.73	9 May	C. Blimp		5.00		205.00
9 May	Sales			95.60		9 May	Wages			80.00	
10 May	N. Smith		4.15		220.50	10 May	A. Hazel		1.50		75.50
11 May	D. Baker		1.87		84.62	11 May	Rates				86.25
12 May	Sales			221.40		12 May	Insurance				42.60
13 May	W. Bolton		4.20		195.80	14 May	Postage			20.14	
14 May	Sales			262.30		14 May	Balances	c/d		642.92	1,020.02
			23.99	1,101.53	1,926.15				15.72	1,101.53	1,926.15
15 May	Balances	b/d	GL 21	642.92	1,020.02				GL 27		

brought down to continue these accounts. However, the column
for discount received is totalled. This is because it is not a proper
account but merely a memorandum or supplementary record.
The total for the first fortnight in May is entered in the account
proper for discount received. The reference beneath the total of
£15.72 tells you that this account will be found on page 27 of the
general ledger. The entry in that account will look like this:

Dr	Discount received	GL 27	Cr
			£
	14 May Sundry creditors		15.72

The debits corresponding to this one total credit will be in the
accounts of the various suppliers from whom discount was
received from 1 to 14 May. These were Thomas, Rees, Robson,
Blimp and Hazel. The end result is still the same in that the total
value of the debits equals the total value of the credit entry in the
discount received account.

The method of keeping a note of discounts received in a
column of the cash book and then entering a total at regular
intervals in the discount received account in the ledger has an
additional advantage. It keeps the discount received account
shorter.

If you have followed the explanation of the use of the discount
received column you should be able to work out for yourself how
the discount allowed column is used on the debit side of the cash
book. Look first at one transaction involving discount allowed –
that of 4 May. A cheque for £388 has been received from R.
Evans who has paid promptly enough to claim a discount of £12.
This has been deducted by him from the full amount owing
before he makes out the cheque.

Self-check

1 How much would Evans have had to pay if he had not
  paid promptly enough to claim the discount?
2 Calculate the percentage discount which is being allowed
  to Evans.

ANSWERS

1 £400.

2

$$\frac{\text{discount}}{\text{total due}} \times \frac{100}{1} = \frac{12}{400} \times \frac{100}{1} = 3\%.$$

The discount allowed column is also a memorandum and not a proper account. At the end of the period the total for all discounts allowed is added and this total is entered in the account proper.

> *Self-check*
>
> Show the entry in the discount allowed account relating to the transactions from 1 to 14 May. Put as much information in it as you can.

ANSWER

Dr		Discount allowed	GL 21	Cr
		£		
1–15 May	Sundry debtors	23.99		

Note that the reference made beneath the total of the discount allowed in the cash book told you that the discount allowed account could be found on page 21 of the general ledger. The credit entries corresponding to this one debit will be in the accounts of the customers or debtors who have been allowed the discounts. Hence the description 'sundry debtors'.

The discounts we have been referring to so far are known fully as cash discounts in order to distinguish them from trade discounts. The latter is a discount that is allowed by a supplier and received by a customer when they are both involved in the same trade. For example, when I buy materials from the local builders' merchant I pay a higher price than would a builder who was a regular customer. He would receive trade discount whereas I would not. Many such merchants even have separate counters to deal with their two categories of customer. The amount of trade discount given will vary according to the trade. As far as the accounts are concerned it does not concern us. The amount of trade discount is taken off *before* any entries are made.

For example, the catalogue or list price of a bag of cement might be £5.00. A builder receiving 10% trade discount will be charged only £4.50, the 50p trade discount being 10% of £5.00. The merchant will make a credit entry of £4.50 in his sales account and debit the builder's account with the £4.50 due from him. The builder would debit his purchases account and credit the account of the merchant with the amount owed to him. Again only the £4.50 would be shown in the accounts. Trade discount is deducted *before* any entries are made.

Of course this does not mean that there will be no cash discount to be shown in the accounts. The merchant may well allow a small discount of, say, 2% to encourage his customers to pay within a certain time period. If he does then this amount will be recorded in the accounts.

Self-check

ACE Motors, a small garage, purchases on credit an exhaust from Spareparts p.l.c. on 25 May. The catalogue price is £80 but all garages are allowed trade discount of 10%. ACE Motors pay the amount due by cheque on 31 May, which is prompt enough to allow them to deduct a cash discount of 3%. Show the accounts in the books of ACE Motors.

ANSWER

Dr			Spareparts p.l.c.			Cr
		£				£
31 May	Bank	69.84	25 May	Purchases		72.00
31 May	Discount received	2.16				

	Purchases		
25 May	Spareparts	72.00	

	Cash book			
		disc	cash	bank
31 May	Spareparts	2.16		69.84

Note that the purchase of the exhaust on 25 May is recorded net of trade discount. The £8, which is 10% of £80, is deducted before entries are made in the accounts. When payment is made on 31 May the cheque is made out for £72 *less* the cash discount of 3%. Thus the cheque paid is for £69.84. The 3% discount received of £2.16 is shown in the account for Spareparts p.l.c. and also in the memorandum column in the cash book. At some time the latter will be added and a total for discounts received entered in the discounts received account in the ledger.

Single entry cash book

So far we have assumed that businesses will have their accounts kept on a double-entry basis. This is not done, however, by many small businesses where it is felt that the effort involved is not sufficiently rewarded by the advantages gained. These businesses will normally keep only a record of money received and paid in a cash book of one kind or another. Such a system is known as single entry because only one entry is made for each transaction. Where this is done, the cash book becomes of even greater importance because it contains the only record of a transaction. It is possible to gain some of the advantages of a double-entry system while keeping only a cash book if the number of columns is expanded and the receipts and payments of money analysed.

For example the cash book on page 108 is used by a trader who makes all his payments by cheque and who banks all receipts of money each day. As he is liable to the government for VAT he uses two columns for this. The first contains the amounts of VAT he has charged customers to whom he has sold goods. The second contains the amounts he has paid the suppliers who have charged him VAT. Wages are the only other expense regular enough to deserve its own column so all the other expenses are classified as sundries. There is nothing to prevent a larger number of columns being used if there are sufficient items which are regular enough to make this worthwhile.

What you have learnt about the cash book so far should enable you to follow the organisation of the following one if you take it one item at a time. It has been assumed that the rate of VAT is 15%.

Cash book

Receipts	Sales	VAT	Date	Details	Payments	Purchases	Wages	Sundries	VAT
500.00			1 Mar.	Balance b/d					
151.80	132.00	19.80	1 Mar.	J. Smith					
			2 Mar.	B. Jones	115.00	100.00			15.00
			3 Mar.	R. Evans	75.50		75.50		
			4 Mar.	British Rail	24.00			24.00	
193.20	168.00	25.20	4 Mar.	W. Toms					
103.73	90.20	13.53	5 Mar.	M. Morgan	312.80	272.00			40.80
			6 Mar.	T. Lewis	421.43				
			7 Mar.	Balance c/d					
948.73	390.20	58.53			948.73	372.00	75.50	24.00	55.80
421.73			8 Mar.	Balance b/d					

Activity

Design a cash book of your own for any kind of business of which you have knowledge.

RESPONSE

The only things that yours need have in common with the ones we have looked at are: space for date, details, money received and money paid. The rest is up to you.

Review

Enter the following transactions in the three-column cash book of J. Harris and balance it on 14 April.

1 April   Cash balance £67.23; bank balance £191.20.
2 April   Cash sales £138.00.
3 April   Paid £100 cash into bank.
4 April   Paid Bentley £120 by cheque, receiving discount of £3.
5 April   Paid Royce £94 by cheque in full settlement of an amount owing of £100 (balance is discount).
6 April   Cash sales £97.24.
7 April   Received a cheque from W. Barnes for £169.50 to settle an amount due of £178.50 (balance is discount).
8 April   Paid wages in cash £120.80.
9 April   Paid T. Ford £98.00 in cash, having deducted a discount of £4.
10 April Withdrew £75 from bank for use as cash.
11 April R. Hewitt paid £95 in cash, having deducted a discount of £5.
12 April Paid insurance on car by cheque £78.90.
13 April Cash sales £120.62.

ANSWER

Compare your answer with mine on page 110, noting any differences. You should rework any transactions which resulted in entries different to mine and correct them.

Cash book

Dr

Date	Details	Folio	Discount allowed	Cash	Bank
1 April	Balances	b/d		67.23	191.20
2 April	Sales			138.00	
3 April	Cash	c			100.00
6 April	Sales			97.24	169.50
7 April	W. Barnes		9.00	75.00	
10 April	Bank	c		75.00	
11 April	R. Hewitt		5.00	95.00	
13 April	Sales			120.62	
			14.00	593.09	460.70
15 April	Balances	b/d		274.29	92.80

Cr

Date	Details	Folio	Discount received	Cash	Bank
3 April	Bank	c			100.00
4 April	Bentley		3.00		120.00
5 April	Royce		6.00		94.00
8 April	Wages			120.80	
9 April	T. Ford		4.00	98.00	
10 April	Cash	c			75.00
12 April	Car insurance				78.90
14 April	Balances	c/d		274.29	92.80
			13.00	593.09	460.70

Review

Looking at the correct cash book of J. Harris, answer the following questions.

1 To what does 'c' refer in the transactions of 3 and 10 April?
2 What kind of discount is contained in the discount columns of the cash book?
3 What do the balances of 15 April mean?
4 Is it possible to have a balance b/d on the credit side of the cash book? Explain your answer.

ANSWERS

1 *Contra*: this means that the double entry is on the same page of the cash book.
2 Cash discount: this must be distinguished from trade discount which does not appear in the accounts.
3 J. Harris has £274.29 in cash and £92.80 in the bank. They are both debit balances and represent assets to him.
4 Yes, but only in the bank column. The cash column on the credit side cannot be greater than the debit because you cannot make cash payments without having received the cash. It is possible, however, to make payments by cheque without having the necessary money in the account. This occurs when an account is overdrawn – something that should not normally happen unless the bank manager has given his permission.

8 | Documents and journals

In this chapter we are going to look at the main sources of information from which entries are made in the ledger and cash book. Then we will examine the way in which some details may be kept in subsidiary books known as journals. These help to reduce the amount of detail needed in the ledger.

The information from which transactions are entered in a trader's personal accounts is obtained from two main documents – invoices and credit notes. An example of an invoice is shown below.

Invoice

Western Electrical Factors
2 Croft Road
Newton Abbot
Devon   Tel. (096) 613412

Invoice to: Date: 8. 7. 1981
RKL Electrics
6 High Street
Torquay   Invoice No. 1693

Quantity	Description	Unit price	Total
			£ p
160 metres		30p	48.00
850 metres		40p	340.00
Terms: 5% cash discount if payment made within 28 days.			388.00

An invoice is basically a bill sent to a purchaser of goods by the seller. If you examine the above invoice you should be able to answer the following.

Self-check

1 Name the purchaser and the seller of the goods.
2 How much will the purchaser pay if he pays within the stated time?

ANSWERS

1 Western Electrical Factors (WEF) is the seller – it is their invoice which has been sent to RKL Electrics, the buyer.
2 £368.60: 5% cash discount = £19.40

The purchaser, who has received the invoice, will use it to make a record of the transaction in his accounts. The seller, who has sent the invoice, will retain a duplicate copy for the same reason. You should know which ledger accounts will be involved.

Self-check

Give the names of the accounts and the entries to be made in **a** the books of WEF and **b** the books of RKL electrics.

ANSWER

a Sales account – credit; RKL account – debit. **b** Purchases account – debit; WEF account – credit.

Activity

Invoices come in a variety of forms. Try to obtain some for comparison. You will find they will have a number of features in common – the most important of which is that one business is telling one of its customers that a certain amount of money is owed to them.

The second important document which relates to buying and selling is the credit note, an example of which is shown overleaf.

Credit notes are frequently printed in red to distinguish them from invoices. They are sent to the purchaser by the seller when goods which have been invoiced are returned. The seller will keep a duplicate copy of the credit note for his own records.

Credit note

Western Electrical Factors
2 Croft Road
Newton Abbot
To: Devon   Tel. (096) 613412
RKL Electrics   Date: 15. 7. 1981
6 High Street   Credit note No. 312
Torquay

Quantity	Description	Unit price	Total
			£ p
160 metres		30p	48.00
			48.00

Self-check

Name the business which has returned the goods referred to in the above credit note.

ANSWER

RKL Electrics has returned the goods. The credit note has been sent to them by WEF. We dealt with returns in Chapter 5 so you should be able to work out which accounts will be involved.

Self-check

From the credit note, give the names of the accounts and the entries to be made in the books of **a** WEF and **b** RKL.

ANSWER

a Sales returns a/c – debit; RKL a/c – credit. Note that from the viewpoint of WEF, the return is something that has previously been sold by them. An alternative which would be acceptable to sales returns is returns inward a/c. The term 'credit note' comes from the fact that the seller is telling the buyer that the buyer's account has been credited by the value of the goods returned.

b WEF a/c – debit; purchases returns a/c – credit. From RKL's point of view the goods they returned could alternatively be entered in an account called returns outward.

Another document connected with buying and selling is the statement. This is a summary of the amounts on all invoices and credit notes sent during a period – normally a month. It shows the purchaser the total amount due from him as a result of all the transactions made. It should be possible for you to obtain a copy of such a document. If you have difficulty refer to a commerce textbook, where you should be able to find a specimen.

When money is paid or received different documents are involved. Payments made by cheque will be entered on the credit side of the cash book from the cheque counterfoils which should be completed each time a cheque is written. Money received by cheque will be entered on the debit side of the cash book using the cheque itself as the document. When payment is made in cash a receipt should be obtained by the payer from which an entry on the credit side of the cash book is made. A business receiving cash should keep a duplicate of the receipt given to the payer, from which debit entries can be made in the cash book.

Self-check

1 Which of the following documents are used to record transactions by **a** the purchaser and **b** the seller? Invoice; duplicate copy of an invoice; credit note; duplicate copy of a credit note.

2 Which of these documents is used to record transactions by **a** the receiver of money and **b** the payer? Cheque; cheque counterfoil; receipt; copy of receipt.

ANSWERS

1 **a** Invoice and credit note. These are sent by the seller to the purchaser.

  b Duplicates of the invoice and credit note. These are retained by the seller for his records.

2 **a** Cheque and copy of receipt.

  b Cheque counterfoil and receipt.

If you had difficulty with this self-check, reread the first part of this chapter.

We will now consider the use of journals – a term meaning a daily record. At one time all transactions were entered in detail in a journal before being posted to the ledger and because of this journals were frequently referred to as the books of original entry. 'Posting to the ledger' is a phrase used to describe the process of making entries in the ledger and does not involve the post office!

The journals are also known as subsidiary books. This is because they are subsidiary or secondary to the ledger. In other words they supplement the ledger. They are not part of the double-entry system itself but relieve the ledger of much unnecessary detail. We have already come across an occasion on which two ledger accounts can be saved too much detail. Do you remember? If not turn to page 103 and look at the three-column cash book. The columns for discount allowed and discount received were used as memorandum records and were not in themselves part of the double-entry system. At the end of a certain period the columns were added and the totals entered in their respective ledger accounts. This considerably reduced the information contained in the accounts for discount allowed and received.

Today few firms would consider it worthwhile to enter all transactions in a journal before making the ledger entries. Journals are still used, however, to keep detailed records of some transactions. The five main ones are:

- The sales journal.
- The sales returns or returns inward journal.
- The purchases journal.
- The purchases returns or returns outward journal.
- The journal.

The first four are kept for credit transactions involving sales, purchases and returns. You should note that 'day book' or 'book' often replaces 'journal', so do not be confused if you encounter a sales day book or returns outward book. The fifth – *the* journal – is often pronounced with emphasis on the first word to distinguish it from other journals. It is sometimes referred to as 'the journal proper' for the same reason. It is used for a number of different transactions when it is felt that extra detail needs to be recorded. Before we consider the way these journals can be used let's make certain you understand what has been said about them so far.

Self-check

1 Are journals part of the double-entry system of book-keeping?
2 What descriptive term indicates that details were recorded in journals before entries were made in the ledger?
3 What term is used to describe the process of making entries in ledger accounts from the journals?
4 State two other possible names for the sales day book.
5 State five other possible names for the purchases returns book.

ANSWERS

1 No – they are subsidiary or supplementary to it.
2 Books of original entry.
3 Posting to the ledger.
4 Sales book, sales journal.
5 Purchases returns day book, purchases returns journal, returns outward day book, returns outward book, returns outward journal.

Reread the preceding section if these questions cause you difficulty.

We will now consider each of the journals in turn. WEF, the electrical wholesalers used as an illustration earlier, can be used again here.

The sales book

All credit sales will be entered here from the duplicate copies of the invoices sent to customers. WEF's sales book could look like this:

		Sales book		28
Date	Customer	Invoice	Folio	£ p
1 July	Robinsons	1690	DL 147	77.50
4 July	Carter and Son	1691	DL 12	31.20
5 July	Allens DIY	1692	DL 6	80.80
6 July	RKL Electrics	1693	DL 152	388.00
7 July	Electroshop	1694	DL 21	163.12
7 July	Transferred to sales a/c		GL 21	740.62

You might be able to follow this but, if not, some explanation
will help. Each customer to whom WEF sells will have his own
personal account in the debtors' ledger. This assumes that WEF
subdivides its ledger. If not the folio reference of DL will be
replaced by GL for general ledger or perhaps simply L for
ledger. The debit entries are made in each customer's personal
account from the duplicate of the invoice as soon as the invoice is
sent. Instead of making a credit entry each time in the sales
account, the entries are saved up and one entry is made at a
convenient time to correspond to the total number of debits
which have been made in the customers' accounts. In the above
example one credit entry for £740.62 on 7 July will be the double
entry corresponding to the five debits from 1 July to 7 July in the
customers' accounts. The sales account will look like this:

Sales account		GL 21	Cr
			£
7 July	Sundry debtors	SB 28	740.62

Note the cross-reference to the sales book and the description
which indicates that several different debtors' accounts are
involved.

The delay in posting the credit entry to the sales account
means that a trial balance extracted between 1 July and 6 July
will not agree. This is because debit entries have been made
without a corresponding credit entry. Book-keepers must be

aware of the effect of keeping subsidiary books on the accuracy of a trial balance. They should choose carefully the date on which they draft it.

The returns inward book

This can take the same form as the sales book and if you have followed the explanation above you should be able to draft your own.

Exercise

The following is a list of the credit sales' returns received by WEF during July.

6 July   Robinsons   £50.12
15 July RKL   £48.00
24 July Evans DIY   £6.54
30 July Walters   £22.12

Enter them in a suitably drawn returns inward book and show the transfer to the ledger account on 31 July. You should invent suitable details.

ANSWER

Returns inward book   3

1981	Customer	Credit note	Folio	£ p
6 July	Robinsons	217	DL 147	50.12
15 July	RKL	218	DL 152	48.00
24 July	Evans DIY	219	DL 24	6.54
30 July	Walters	220	DL 189	22.12
31 July	Transferred to returns inward a/c		GL 22	126.78

Dr		Returns inward account	GL 22
		£	
31 July	Sundry debtors RIB 3	126.78	

Did you remember that the document involved this time would be the credit note and not the invoice? If so, well done! If you were really awake you may have used the same folio reference numbers for Robinsons and RKL as were used in the sales book. The credit note reference numbers and the other folios would have to have been invented. You should now be able to answer the following to show that you understand what has been done.

> *Self-check*
>
> 1 What kind of entry will have been made in each of the customers' accounts?
> 2 On what date will the entry have been made in Robinsons' account?

ANSWERS

1 A credit entry will have been made in each customer's account to reduce the balance owing by the value of the goods returned to WEF. Remember, the credit note is so called because the seller is informing his customers that he has credited their accounts. The total of these credits correspond to the debit entry of £126.78 made in the returns inward a/c.
2 6 July – the date the credit note was sent.

The purchases book

This contains all the credit purchases. It will be made up from the invoices received from suppliers. WEF's purchases book might look like this:

Purchases book   8

1981	Supplier	Invoice	Folio	£ p
3 July	Wireplies	82/101	CL 29	289.50
16 July	UVC	82/102	CL 17	341.38
17 July	Plugplies	82/103	CL 22	429.17
24 July	Jones	82/104	CL 14	121.12
29 July	Electose	82/105	CL 7	321.03
31 July	Transferred to purchases a/c		GL 16	1,502.20

Each of WEF's suppliers have a personal account in the creditors' ledger. The credit entries are made in each of these accounts from an invoice as soon as it is received. The debit entries are saved up and one entry is made to correspond to the total number of credits which will have been made already in the suppliers' accounts. In the above example one debit entry of £1,502.20 is made on 31 July in the purchases account which will look like this:

Dr			Purchases account	GL 16
			£	
31 July	Sundry creditors	PB 8	1,502.20	

Note that the invoices received from suppliers will have a variety of reference numbers. To aid filing, WEF has stamped each one with its own number which is used in the purchases book.

Self-check

If WEF extracted a trial balance from its ledger accounts on 20 July, would it balance?

ANSWER

No! On that date there will be amounts in the purchases book (and other books of original entry) which will have been entered in the personal accounts but not in the other ledger accounts. A trial balance should be drawn up only after all double entries have been completed.

The returns outward book

This can take the same form as the others and you should be able to draft your own.

Exercise

The following is a list of the credit notes received by WEF during July:

		£ p
8 July	EQP Ltd	38.29
10 July	Electose	49.54
23 July	Plugplies	56.20
28 July	Jones	17.47
29 July	Wilsons	38.25

Enter these in a returns outward book and show the transfer to the ledger account on 31 July. Invent suitable details.

ANSWER

Returns outward book   6

1981	Supplier	Credit note	Folio	£ p
8 July	EQP Ltd	82/24	CL 9	38.29
10 July	Electose	82/25	CL 7	49.54
23 July	Plugplies	82/26	CL 22	56.20
28 July	Jones	82/27	CL 14	17.47
29 July	Wilsons	82/28	CL 27	38.25
31 July	Transferred to returns outward a/c		GL 17	199.75

GL 17 Returns outward account   Cr

		£
31 July Sundry creditors ROB 6		199.75

To save space the examples used have been fairly brief. The real value of removing much of the detail from ledger accounts like sales, purchases, returns inward and returns outward into journals is seen when the number of entries is very large. Not all firms, however large, will keep separate day books. A good filing system for copies of invoices sent (sales), invoices received (purchases), copies of credit notes sent (returns inward) and credit notes received (returns outward) may well suffice. It will still enable total entries for sales, purchases, returns inward and returns outward to be made at regular intervals while the entries in the personal accounts are made as the transactions occur.

The journal

At one time this was used to record transactions that did not have their own book of original entry. As well as the four books we have just dealt with the cash book is also considered to be a book of original entry in this context because entries are made in it directly from documents such as cheques. The cash book differs, however, in that it is also part of the ledger as it contains two ledger accounts – cash and bank.

Today the journal is usually reserved for those transactions that need extra explanation. Its form is the same as the day books we have just examined but the columns are used differently. The standard layout is like this:

Journal

Date		Folio	£ dr	£ cr
	Name of the a/c to be debited. Name of the a/c to be credited. The narrative or explanation.			

Let's see how some transactions that might be entered in the journal would fit into this layout.

The purchase or sale of a fixed asset on credit

On 28 January, WEF purchased a Mini-van registration no. OAF 691X on credit from Apex Garages for £2,500.

Journal

			£ dr	£ cr
28 Jan.	Motor vehicle a/c	GL 9	2,500	
	Apex Garages a/c	GL 22		2,500
	Purchase of mini-van reg. no. OAF 691X			

Opening a set of ledger accounts

On 1 May, N. Couch started in business with capital of £2,000 consisting of £1,800 in the bank and £200 cash.

Journal

			£ dr	£ cr
1 May	Cash a/c	CB 1	200	
	Bank a/c	CB 1	1,800	
	Capital a/c	GL 1		2,000
	Assets and capital at the start of business		2,000	2,000

In this case, because there is more than one debit, the entries
have been totalled. This was not done in the first example
because it can be seen immediately that the value of one debit
entry equals the value of the other credit entry. Entries in the
journal cover a great variety of transactions and it is necessary
only to draw a line beneath one before writing the next. Of
course the entries must still be made in the ledger accounts
themselves.

Writing off a bad debt

On 12 April, G. Thomas died owing £12 to WEF. The firm wrote
off the debt when it was discovered that he died penniless.

Journal

			£ dr	£ cr
26 April	Bad debts a/c	GL 28	12	
	G. Thomas a/c	DL 13		12
	Debt written off owing to death of G. Thomas			

As you can see, there is nothing difficult about doing the journal
entries. Provided that you understand the rules of double-entry
book-keeping it is merely a question of fitting the information
into the right boxes. The advantage is that more information can
be given in the journal narrative than in the details column of the

ledger. Remember, however, that the entries must still be made in the ledger accounts themselves.

Self-check

Enter the following transaction in the journal to make certain you have grasped the layout.

9 May, WEF sold an electronic typewriter (serial no. 68/54321) valued in the books at £600 for this amount to Southern Electrical Factors on credit.

ANSWER

Journal

			£ dr	£ cr

9 May	Southern Electrical Factors a/c
	          Office equipment a/c
	Sale of electronic typewriter
	  serial no. 68/54321
		DL 4
		
		CL 6
			600	600

Review

1 Write definitions of invoice, credit note and statement.
2 List the five books of original entry dealt with in this chapter, giving an alternative name for each.
3 Say whether the following statement is true or false: Journals are valuable because they reduce the number of entries required in the ledger and provide a place where the details of transactions can be recorded.

ANSWERS

The answer to question 3 is 'true'. The other questions can be checked by referring back to the text.

9 | Introducing control

In this chapter we are going to examine two very important matters. The first involves the money in the bank and the second concerns the personal accounts of debtors and creditors. Control is really a function of management accounting and as such might seem beyond the scope of this book. Our task here, therefore, will be to take an introductory look at the idea of control. It is assumed you are fully acquainted with the cash book and the divisions of the ledger which were looked at in Chapter 7.

Bank reconciliation statements

If you have a current account with a bank, you may have received a statement showing a balance in the bank considerably different to what you expected it to be. Your delight or dismay (depending on the nature of the difference) at the amount shown will probably have disappeared once you sat down and worked out the reasons for the difference. If you write up a cash book yourself in order to keep a check on your spending (and by this stage in the book it is to be hoped that you do!) then accounting for the difference should not be too difficult. In a big business where there have been a large number of entries to record money received and paid it may take a little longer. The principles are the same however detailed the account. Once mastered you should have no problems explaining or 'reconciling' (the technical term) the differences between your record and that of the bank.

In reconciling the bank balance in the cash book with the balance in the bank statement, it is possible that you will uncover errors made by either yourself or the bank. This is the main object in drafting a bank reconciliation statement. Correcting such errors when they are discovered is essential.

For the sake of those readers who do not have a current account we will begin by looking at the bank statement below which is a fairly typical specimen.

Lloyds Bank		Description of entries		
Torre branch		BGC Bank giro credit		
		DIV Dividend		
A/c No: 4623610 *Valuemart*		D/D Direct debit		
		S/O Standing order		
		Cheques are designated by the serial number.		

Date	Particulars		Payments	Receipts	Balance
1982	Opening balance				146.12
14 May	Sundry credit			200.60	346.72
17 May		004520	21.98		
		004521	100.26		224.48
18 May	Sundry credit			300.25	
		004524	19.90		
		004526	44.20		460.63
20 May	Bank giro credit			280.62	
		004522	20.62		
		004527	220.14		
		004529	16.21		484.28
21 May	Sundry credit			461.90	
	Alpha Insurance S/O		46.80		
		004528	315.20		
		004530	16.29		567.89

Activity

Make sure you are fully conversant with the terms used in the bank statement.

RESPONSE

If you were uncertain of any of these terms, e.g. the difference between bank giro credit and sundry credit, you could have inquired at your local bank.

You should be able to give a good account of what has been happening in Valuemart's current account in the week covered by the account. For example you can state that the balance *before* business began on 14 May was £146.12 and that as a result of £200.60 being put into the account the balance grew to £346.72. After two cheques had been cleared for payment on 17 May the balance fell to £224.48. It is impossible to give any more detail about the transactions. For instance you cannot say to whom cheque no. 004520 was paid. To obtain this kind of information you would need access to Valuemart's cash book or the documents, such as cheque counterfoils, from which it is prepared. To assist you the relevant parts of the cash book have been reproduced opposite. To simplify matters the columns for cash and discounts have been omitted. The owner uses the folio column on the credit side to record the reference numbers of the cheques he has written.

Self-check

Spend some time comparing the structure of the statement kept by the bank with that of the cash book kept by the owner of Valuemart. Do not concern yourself with each individual entry but concentrate on obtaining a general picture of the differences between them. It may help you to make a note of these.

ANSWER

You have probably noticed the following:

- Only one date and one details column are used in the bank statement.
- In the bank statement the receipts column containing amounts deposited into the bank is to the right of the payments column which contains the amounts paid by cheque, standing orders, etc. In the cash book the receipts are shown as debits and the payments as credits, exactly the other way around. This was explained in Chapter 4, page 46, and it may help you to refer back to it now.
- In the bank statement a running balance is shown after each day's transactions. This is easy for them as their records are computerised.
- Although the opening balance is the same in each account the balance differs on 21 May.

Cash book

Dr					Date		Ch. no.	Cr
Date			£ p					£ p
14 May	Balance	b/d	146.12		14 May	Health Foods Ltd	4520	21.98
14 May	Cash sales		200.60		14 May	Tresco C&C	4521	100.26
18 May	Cash sales		300.25		15 May	Electricity Board	4522	20.62
19 May	Cash sales		280.62		15 May	Advertising – *Echo*	4523	18.50
21 May	Cash sales		461.90		16 May	Vehicle expenses	4524	19.90
					16 May	Rates	4525	105.25
					16 May	Johnsons	4526	44.20
					17 May	Tresco C&C	4527	220.14
					17 May	Bilby Vintners	4528	315.20
					17 May	Evans	4529	16.21
					17 May	Sibsons	4530	16.29
					20 May	Yeos	4531	10.80
					21 May	Balance	c/d	480.14
			1,389.49					1,389.49
22 May	Balance	b/d	480.14					

We will now turn to reconciling or explaining the different balances which exist on 21 May. If the records of the two parties to the current account – the bank and the owner of Valuemart – result in a different balance being shown there are two reasons why this may have happened.

First, and most likely, one party may not know what the other party has done, or possibly it was known but has been forgotten. The most common example of this surrounds the writing of cheques. The account holder is able to record a payment by cheque in the cash book on the day he writes the cheque. His bank will learn of this only when the cheque is presented for payment. This will take a few days even when the receiver pays it into his own bank immediately. If he holds on to it for a while, this increases the time that the bank will be out of step with the client's cash book. It is also possible that the account holder will lack knowledge of a transaction completed by his bank. For example, it is normal practice not to invoice clients for the charges due for operating the account. A deduction is made from the account and the client learns of this only when he receives his next statement. In addition many people forget that they have completed a form permitting their bank to make payments for them by standing order or direct debit. The arrival of the statement serves as a timely reminder.

The second reason for a discrepancy in the balances is that an error has been made by either one party or the other.

The sooner errors are discovered, the sooner they can be corrected. This is why bank reconciliation is so important. To illustrate the best way of approaching it, we will reconcile Valuemart's cash book balance in the bank statement on 21 May. There are three main steps:

1 Compare the cash book with the bank statement, noting any differences. It is useful to tick each entry in the cash book that is also in the statement and each entry in the statement that is also in the cash book. The entries not ticked will help to explain why the balances are different.

Self-check

Use the above method to find the differences and write them down.

ANSWER

In the cash book the payments by cheques numbered 4523, 4525 and 4531 will not be ticked and in the bank statement the payment to Alpha Insurance by standing order. It is advisable to write down these differences clearly:

In the cash book but not in the statement
15 May   £18.50 paid for advertising by cheque no. 4523.
16 May   £105.25 paid for rates by cheque no. 4525.
20 May   £10.80 paid to Yeos by cheque no. 4531.

In the statement but not in the cash book
22 May   £46.80 paid to Alpha Insurance by standing order.

2 The next step is to **bring the cash book up to date** by entering any items which are not yet included but which are in the statement.

Self-check

Bring Valuemart's cash book up to date. Note there is no need to rewrite the cash book.

ANSWER

		Cash book			
		£			£
22 May	Balance b/d	480.14	22 May	Alpha Insurance	46.80

You should have made the entry for the payment by standing order on the credit side of the cash book. Remember, from Valuemart's point of view this shows the reduction of an asset. You are now able to tick this entry in both cash book and bank statement. The bank balance as shown in the cash book now stands at £433.34, i.e. £480.14 less £46.80. Sometimes this is all that has to be done to reconcile it with the bank statement. We know that on this occasion there is still more to be done.

3 The final step is to **draft a brief statement** to reconcile the differences which remain. Here is the normal method:

Bank reconciliation statement 22 May 1982

		£	£
Balance (amended) as per cash book			433.34
add Back cheques not presented			
	4523	18.50	
	4525	105.25	
	4531	10.80	
			134.55
Balance as per bank statement			567.89

The cheques are added back to the cash book balance because the bank statement will be that much *greater* because they have not yet been deducted from Valuemart's account. The above statement achieves its purpose in that it successfully accounts for the differences between the two balances. If the two balances had not been reconciled by this process, the errors would have to be located and corrected. Bank reconciliation statements are usually filed with the bank statements for future reference.

Exercise

A trader checked his cash book against the bank statement dated 31 July. He listed the following discrepancies:

- Balance as per CB £456.71; balance as per BS £182.78.
- Cheques written by him but not yet presented for payment: no. 2179 for £20.50; no. 2181 for £5.32; no. 2184 for £65.74.
- His takings of £300 on 31 July had been banked late in the day and were not shown in the statement.
- Payment had been made to Grampian Insurance for £48.25 by direct debit.
- Bank charges £17.24.

First bring the cash book balance up to date by entering those transactions which would be in the statement but not yet included in the cash book. Then draft a bank reconciliation statement to account for the remaining differences between the bank statement balance and the amended cash book balance.

ANSWER

Dr		£	Cash book		Cr £
31 July	Balance b/d	456.71	31 July	Bank charges	17.24
			31 July	Grampian Insurance	48.25

The trader would not have known the amount of the bank charges until he received his statement. He should have known that he had completed a direct debit form for payments to be made to Grampian Insurance but it is the type of transaction often overlooked. In addition, the amount to be paid could vary and he would know this only when receiving the statement. The amended cash book balance will now be £391.22.

Bank reconciliation statement 31 July 1982

		£	£
Balance (amended) as per cash book			391.22
add Back cheques not presented	2179	20.50	
	2181	5.32	
	2184	65.74	
			91.56
			482.78
deduct Cash takings not yet entered by the bank			300.00
Balance as per bank statement			182.78

The only difference between this and the example we looked at is the cash takings. Since the trader has entered this in his cash book but the bank has not done so in its records the statement balance will be that much *less* than the cash book balance. Deducting this amount from the trader's amended cash book balance should therefore give us the same balance as in the bank statement. As it does, we can assume there are no errors.

Sales ledger and purchases ledger control accounts

In Chapter 6 we saw how a trial balance could be used to check the accuracy of transactions made in the ledger. This process can be extended by checking individual sections of the ledger, such as the sales or debtors' ledger and purchases or creditors' ledger. It is especially useful for firms with large numbers of debtors and creditors, where the chances of error are greater. In such firms it is likely that the sales and purchases ledgers will be sectionalised.

As an illustration we will assume that Jill is responsible for a firm's sales ledger containing the accounts of customers with names in the range A–D. She will have to make a large number of debit entries for sales and credits for payments received, discounts allowed, returns accepted and perhaps bad debts written off. Look at one of the debtor accounts earlier in the book to remind you of what would be included. At the end of April the debit balances in her customers' accounts totalled £12,984. We can tell if this is correct by obtaining all the information referring to her customers and entering it into one account as follows.

Dr			Sales ledger (A–D) control account		Cr
		£			£
1 April	Balances b/d	13,621	1–30 April	Cash	465
1–30 April	Sales	16,200	1–30 April	Bank	15,000
			1–30 April	Discount allowed	324
			1–30 April	Returns in	944
			1–30 April	Bad debts	104
			30 April	Balances c/d	12,984
		29,821			29,821
1 May	Balance b/d	12,984			

This account could also be known as the total debtors (A–D) control account. This is because it contains as totals all the entries referring to debtors (A–D). It is not part of the double-entry system but is kept outside it as a memorandum account.

You can see that when Jill's balances from her sales ledger are inserted on to the credit side (ready to be brought down to the debit side where they belong), the totals of the account £29,821 agree. This would be accepted as sufficient proof that there are no errors in Jill's section of the sales ledger. Suppose, however, the balances in her section totalled £12,274 on 30 April. The control account with this inserted would be as follows.

Dr			Sales ledger (A–D) control account		Cr
		£			£
1 April	Balances b/d	13,621	1–30 April	Cash	465
1–30 April	Sales	16,200	1–30 April	Bank	15,000
			1–30 April	Discounts allowed	324
			1–30 April	Returns inward	944
			1–30 April	Bad debts	104
			30 April	Balances c/d	12,274
		29,821			29,111

Clearly something is wrong in this section of the sales ledger. The error(s) will have to be traced and corrected as soon as possible. If this control account had not been kept the error(s) would not have been revealed until the trial balance was prepared. This would give no guidance as to which accounts in it were at fault.

Self-check

From the following information about the sales ledger (E–H) prepare a control account on 30 April and state whether it reveals any errors.

		£
1 April	Debit balances	15,321
1–30 April	Total credit sales	18,640
1–30 April	Total cash received	720
1–30 April	Total cheques received	12.930

1–30 April	Total discounts allowed	380
1–30 April	Bad debts	206
1–30 April	Total returns inward	621
1–30 April	Debit balances obtained from sales ledger	19,104

ANSWER

Dr			Sales ledger (E–H) control account		Cr
		£			£
1 April	Balances b/d	15,321	1–30 April	Cash	720
1–30 April	Sales	18,640	1–30 April	Bank	12,930
			1–30 April	Discounts allowed	380
			1–30 April	Returns inward	621
			1–30 April	Bad debts	206
			30 April	Balances c/d	19,104
		33,961			33,961
1 May	Balances b/d	19,104			

As the totals agree, no error is revealed.

The figures for the sales ledger control account should be obtained from original entries. To do this easily the sales book and returns inward book should have analysis columns to match the sections of the ledger covered by the individual clerks. It will help also if the cash book is analysed in this way as the entries for cash and cheques received as well as discounts allowed will be obtained from that source. Entries for bad debts will be obtained from the journal which is not analysed. However, as such entries are comparatively few, it should not take too long to go through this book and extract the entries relevant to each of the sections of the sales ledger.

The purchases ledger can be controlled in a similar manner. It will, of course, differ because it contains the accounts of suppliers. In these accounts the balances will be credit balances and there will be credit entries for goods bought on credit. The debit entries in these accounts will be for amounts paid by cash or cheque, discounts received and returns outward. Remind yourself about the contents of a creditor's account by referring to one earlier in the book.

The principles involved in constructing a purchases ledger control account are the same as for the sales ledger. Similarly, it may be known as the total creditors' control account. You should therefore be able to tackle the following.

> ### Exercise
>
> Prepare a control account from the following information which refers to the purchases ledger (A–M).
>
> | | | £ |
> |---|---|---|
> | 1 April | Credit balances | 27,431 |
> | 1–30 April | Total goods bought on credit | 82,500 |
> | 1–30 April | Total cash paid | 462 |
> | 1–30 April | Total cheques paid | 84,160 |
> | 1–30 April | Total goods returned | 468 |
> | 1–30 April | Total discounts received | 1,605 |
> | 30 April | Credit balances obtained from purchases ledger | 23,236 |

ANSWER

Dr	Purchases ledger (A–M) control account				Cr
		£			£
1–30 April	Cash	462	1 April	Balances b/d	27,431
1–30 April	Bank	84,160	1–30 April	Purchases	82,500
1–30 April	Discounts rec.	1,605			
1–30 April	Returns outward	468			
30 April	Balances c/d	23,236			
		109,931			109,931
			1 May	Balances b/d	23,236

To obtain information easily the books of original entry should be analysed in the same manner in which the purchases ledger is subdivided. This will involve the purchases book, returns outward book and the credit side of the cash book.

As the purchases ledger control account contains total figures covering all the accounts in the purchases ledger it is possible that there will be some debit balances included. How can a ledger

containing the accounts of suppliers to whom money is owed
contain debit balances? The answer is that it is possible for
returns to be made *after* goods have been paid for. Thus, for a
short time, the suppliers will owe the purchaser for the amount of
the returns. Such accounts will be relatively small, as can be seen
from the following example.

Dr		£	Purchases ledger control account		Cr £
1 May	Balances b/d	200	1 May	Balances b/d	20,600
1–31 May	Bank	68,720	1–31 May	Purchases	72,000
1–31 May	Discounts rec.	14,830	1–31 May	Balances c/d	180
1–31 May	Returns inward	641			
31 May	Balances c/d	8,389			
		92,780			92,780
1 June	Balances b/d	180	1 June	Balances b/d	8,389

At both the beginning and end of the month the credit balances
are much bigger than the debit balances, as you would expect in a
ledger containing the accounts of suppliers.

It is common also for the sales ledger to have a number of
accounts with temporary credit balances. These will be the
accounts of customers who have returned goods after having
paid for them. Eventually they will purchase more goods and the
credit balances will be set off against these purchases. The
majority of the accounts in the sales ledger will, of course, have
debit balances.

Exercise

Write up a sales ledger control account from the following
information.

		£
1 May	Debit balances in sales ledger	24,860
1 May	Credit balances in sales ledger	190
31 May	Debit balances in sales ledger	28,140
31 May	Credit balances in sales ledger	240
1–31 May	Cheques received from customers	86,420
1–31 May	Discount allowed to customers	1,730
1–31 May	Returns inward	960
1–31 May	Sales on credit	92,340

ANSWER

Dr		Sales ledger control account			Cr
		£			£
1 May	Balances b/d	24,860	1 May	Balances b/d	190
1–31 May	Sales	92,340	1–31 May	Bank	86,420
31 May	Balances c/d	240	1–31 May	Discounts allowed	1,730
			1–31 May	Returns inward	960
			31 May	Balances c/d	28,140
		117,440			117,440
1 June	Balances b/d	28,140	1 June	Balances b/d	240

We have assumed that the sales ledger and purchases ledger control account are being kept outside the double-entry system. It is possible for them to become an integral part of that system. However, if this is done the personal accounts must be regarded as outside the system otherwise some entries would be appearing twice.

Review

1 Give reasons why the bank balance in the cash book differs from that in the bank statement at the same date.

2 Give the three stages involved in reconciling the bank balance as per the cash book with that in the bank statement.

3 State the sources from which entries will be made in **a** the sales ledger control account; **b** the purchases ledger control account.

ANSWERS

1 The most common are: cheques not presented for payment, bank charges, standing orders, direct debits and cheques paid into the bank which have not yet been cleared. It is also possible that one party or both may have made a mistake.
2 The three stages are:
   a Compare the cash book and bank statement and list the differences.
   b Bring the cash book up to date by entering those differences which are in the statement but not yet in the cash book.
   c Draft a reconciliation statement to explain the remaining differences.
3 **a** Sales book, returns inward book, cash book, journal and the sales ledger itself.
   b Purchases book, returns outward book, cash book and the purchases ledger itself.

10 | Measuring profit

The main theme of the remainder of this book can be summed up by one word: profit. It is something of vital importance to all businesses. In this chapter we will examine concepts which are essential to understanding how to measure profit. In the next chapter we will deal with the method of measurement and in the remaining chapters with particular problems relating to its measurement.

We will begin with a simple definition:

- *The profit made by a business is the difference between the total income or revenue earned and the total expenses incurred during a particular period of time.*

The trouble with a simple definition is that it often hides a number of difficulties, and this one is no exception. Let's explore some of them.

The actual period of time chosen is not a major problem. The owner may decide to see how much profit he has made in the last six months, three months, week, day or in any period that he chooses. However, in order to meet the requirements of the Inland Revenue, which assesses the tax that he has to pay on his profits, it is necessary for him to provide information on an annual basis. In fact most small businesses measure their profits at yearly or, at most, six-monthly intervals.

The calculation itself is not especially difficult – though the above definition does fail to make one thing absolutely clear. Can you think what it is? If not, the following self-check will assist you.

Self-check

Calculate the profit made in the following circumstances.

a April – income earned, £2,000; expenses incurred, £1,500.

b May – income earned, £2,200; expenses incurred, £2,600.

ANSWER

a Profit in April = £500.

b In May a *loss* of £400 has been suffered. This is what the definition fails to make absolutely clear: where earnings are less than expenses, profit is *negative*. In practice the term 'loss' is more frequently used.

The main problem is not, then, one of the time period chosen nor is it the actual calculation. It lies, rather, in the need to answer the questions: What counts as expenses incurred? And what counts as income or revenue earned? To answer the first question correctly it is necessary for you to understand the distinction between capital and revenue expenditure.

Capital and revenue expenditure

Capital expenditure is expenditure on acquiring fixed assets. These are those assets which are bought to last the business a long time and which help to make profits over that period. You should be able to list some examples of fixed assets as they were mentioned earlier in this volume. If you cannot remember, a glance at the balance sheet on page 28 should help. When you are happy that you can give some examples of fixed assets, consider this: would it be fair to take the cost of buying such an asset, which will last for several years, from the earnings of only one year? Clearly the answer is 'no'. Therefore it would be wrong to include the purchase of a fixed asset or capital expenditure in the calculation of one year's profit.

Revenue expenditure is the spending which relates to benefits which do not last for longer than one year. Expenditure on all items except the purchase of fixed assets can therefore be regarded as revenue expenditure. You should be able to think of some examples but if you find it difficult look back to Chapter 5, where we considered how such expenses should be entered in the ledger. Since expenditure of this nature is directly related to the earning of revenue it is quite correct that it should be deducted from revenue when calculating profit.

Self-check

Judy Brooks recently opened a restaurant. Some of her items of expenditure are listed below. Complete the table by putting a tick in those columns which are relevant to each item.

Items of expenditure	Capital	Revenue	Used in measuring profit
a Purchase of premises			
b Wages			
c Insurance			
d Purchase of equipment			
e Gas and electricity			
f Purchase of china			
g Advertising			
h Repairs to equipment			

ANSWER

You should have ticked both the revenue and the profit columns for **b**, **c**, **e**, **g** and **h**. These are examples of revenue expenditure. They do not provide a fixed asset to last for a long period of time and therefore must be included in calculating the profits of the business each year. Item **h** should be carefully noted. Repairs are defined as expenditure which restores an asset to the value at which it stood immediately prior to its needing attention. When a fixed asset is in need of repair it is not considered necessary to show the reduction in its value in its account. Consequently it would be wrong to show its value increasing when the repair has been carried out. Therefore, as a repair does not increase the value of an asset, it should be regarded as revenue expenditure.

Items **a**, **d** and **f** involve expenditure on fixed assets, which are expected to last longer than one year. They are not deducted from one year's income to measure profit therefore and only the capital column should have been ticked.

You must not assume that the distinction between what counts as capital expenditure and as revenue expenditure is always clear cut. We referred earlier (page 67) to the concept of depreciation, which is the reduction in the value of a fixed asset resulting from its use. For example, some kitchen equipment bought by Judy for her restaurant might have an estimated working life of five years. She (or her accountant) might decide that, each year, one fifth of the cost of this equipment should be deducted from that year's profits to allow for its depreciation in value. One fifth of the asset's cost will be removed from the asset account and transferred to an account for depreciation. This depreciation will then be counted as one of the items of revenue expenditure for that year and deducted from the year's income in order to obtain the profit figure. We will consider this in more detail in Chapter 14. For now, it is enough if you recognise that even the purchase of a fixed asset, which counts as capital expenditure, may directly result in an expense which is included in the calculation of profit.

Self-check

At the beginning of 1981, Judy bought a freezer for £320 and she estimated that it would last for eight years.

1 Would you regard this purchase as capital or revenue expenditure?
2 If she decided to allow for depreciation in equal amounts over the estimated life of the freezer, what amount would count as revenue expenditure in the calculation of profit each year?

ANSWERS

1 The purchase is clearly capital expenditure as it results in the acquisition of a fixed asset.
2 Reducing the value of the asset by one eighth each year means that £40 depreciation will count as revenue expenditure. This amount will be deducted from income to calculate profit each year for the following eight years.

Capitalising a revenue expense

Sometimes an expenditure which is normally quite correctly classified as revenue, and recorded as such, is turned into capital expenditure. The most common example involves maintenance workers who spend most of their time repairing and maintaining fixed assets. Their earnings will normally be recorded as a wages account and quite correctly, as an item of revenue expenditure, deducted from each year's income to obtain profit. Occasionally, however, they might be employed to *improve* a fixed asset and not merely to restore its value. If this happens their earnings, while performing this task, should be removed from the wages account, which counts as revenue expenditure, and transferred to an account for the fixed asset which has increased in value.

An example will help to make this clear. The maintenance staff at Tom Brown's engineering works used waste material to build shelves in a storeroom. Their total wages for the period when the shelves were being erected amounted to £250. If this is allowed to remain in the wages account it will be deducted (as part of the total wages paid during the year) from income to obtain profit. Clearly this would not be fair as £250 of the expenditure on wages is resulting in an increase in the value of an asset which will last for some considerable time. The £250 should be transferred from the wages account to an account for fixtures and fittings. As it is a relatively unusual transaction it would probably be recorded in the journal before being posted to the ledger. It is known as the capitalisation of a revenue expense and the journal entry for it is shown below.

		F	dr	cr
28 Feb.	Fixtures and fittings		250	
	Wages account			250
	Being the capitalisation			
	of revenue expenditure on			
	improving the storeroom			

Self-check

Tom's maintenance men are employed later that year to build a storage bunker. They use materials purchased by the business for production purposes worth £400 and while building it are paid wages of £300. Show the journal entries necessary to capitalise the revenue expenditure involved.

ANSWER

Date		F	dr	cr
	Premises	—	700	
	Wages	—		300
	Purchases			400
	Being the capitalisation of revenue expenses in improving the property			

Thus £300 is removed from the wages account and £400 from the purchases (of materials) account. The value of the premises is then increased by £700.

Having considered the distinction between the capital and revenue expenditure we can now turn to the second question posed earlier: what counts as income or revenue earned? The answer to this requires an understanding of the distinction between capital and revenue receipts.

Capital and revenue receipts

A capital receipt is finance invested in a business either by the owner or by an outside firm. Suppose that one year Judy Brooks decided to invest an additional £1,000 of her own money in her restaurant and paid this amount into the business bank account. Would it be fair to include this amount as income or revenue received for that year, from which expenses will be deducted to calculate profit? Clearly not, as the business is not *earning* any revenue but is being given additional finance to use. The entries to show this in the accounts would be: debit entry in the bank account to increase the value of the asset, and a credit entry in the capital account to increase the value of the finance invested by the owner.

Similarly, finance may be received by way of a loan from another person or firm. Suppose Judy borrowed £6,000 by means of a loan from Cityfinance p.l.c. The assets of the business will increase by this amount. Such an increase is not income or revenue earned, however, but simply additional finance borrowed for use in the business. It is therefore regarded as a receipt of capital and not included as income from which expenses are to be deducted to arrive at profit.

> *Self-check*
>
> Assume that the £6,000 loan from Cityfinance is paid into Judy's bank account. Show the ledger entries to record this transaction.

ANSWER

Bank a/c			
	£		
Cityfinance	6,000		

Cityfinance a/c			
	£		
	6,000	Bank	6,000

The debit entry in the bank account (or bank column in the cash book) records the increase in the value of the assets and the credit entry in an account for Cityfinance creates a liability for that amount. The latter is a loan account recording finance invested by an outside firm and *not* an income account which would record revenue or income earned.

It is also possible that the capital of a business will increase as a result of the capitalisation of a revenue expense. Look again at the self-check on page 146. Suppose that the work of Tom

Brown's maintenance men resulted in a storage bunker which increased the value of the premises by £1,000. This is £300 more than the value of the labour and materials employed in the construction. This £300 is not regarded as income or revenue earned from the normal activities of the business because the maintenance men are really employed to carry out repairs to assets. It is considered to represent a direct increase in the value of the business to the owner by means of an increase in the capital of the business. The journal entry to record the capitalisation of the revenue expenditure under these circumstances would be as follows.

		F	dr	cr
Date	Premises		1,000	
	Wages			300
	Purchases			400
	Capital			300
	Being capitalisation of revenue expenses on improving the property			

Revenue or income is money received from the normal profit-making activities of a business. In a business which sells goods, the value of the sales will be the major item of income or revenue. Other businesses, such as accountants or lawyers, receive fees for their services rendered. Whatever the business, it is also possible that some additional income may be received which may be regarded as part of normal trading. For instance, the owner of a shop may let the flat above it and receive rent, or a service may be performed for which commission is received. Such additional income, however, will normally be relatively small in relation to the main profit-making activity of the business.

Having sorted out the meaning of the terms 'capital expenditure', 'revenue expenditure', 'capital receipts' and 'revenue receipts', you should now be quite clear on what to include and what to exclude when calculating profit. Let's see how well you have grasped the points made.

Self-check

First write down the definition of 'profit' with which we started this chapter. Try to do it without looking back. Then say whether each of the following statements is true or false.

a Both capital and revenue expenditure must be included in the calculation of a firm's profit.

b Neither receipts of capital nor receipts of income should be included in the calculation of a firm's profit.

c The purchase of fixtures and fittings is an example of capital expenditure.

d Wages paid to employees are an example of revenue expenditure.

e Repairs to a damaged machine are an example of capital expenditure.

f A legacy received by the owner of a business and invested in the business is an example of a receipt of revenue or income.

g The sale of a car by a car dealer results in the receipt of revenue.

ANSWER

Writing down the definition should have helped you in deciding whether the statements were true or false. Let's remind ourselves of it before we continue.

- *The profit made by a business is the difference between the total income or revenue earned and the total expenses incurred during a particular period of time.*

Statements **c**, **d** and **g** are true; **a** is false because, although revenue expenditure is included, capital expenditure is not; **b** is false because, while receipts of income are included, capital receipts are not; **e** is false because it is assumed that repairs merely restore an asset to its original value before it was damaged: there is thus no increase in the value of the asset; **f** is false because this is an example of a capital receipt.

It is worth summarising the main points of the chapter so far. In measuring profit the emphasis is on income or revenue earned (i.e. revenue receipts) and expenses incurred (i.e. revenue expenditure) during the period for which profit is being measured. In fact our definition of profit could be abbreviated to:

- *revenue receipts* less *revenue expenditure.*

The purchase of a fixed asset – capital expenditure – must not be included because the value will last for longer than one year. The receipt of capital must not be included because it is not derived from the profit-making activity of the business. It is likely that such a receipt is a loan to the business from an outside firm or a further investment of finance in the business by the owner.

Another transaction which occurs frequently and which must not be allowed to affect the calculation of profit is the withdrawal of any of the assets from the business by the owner for his private use. Such a withdrawal is known as 'drawings'. The assets most usually affected are cash or bank. The entries to record such a withdrawal are: credit the asset account and debit the capital account. The credit entry in the asset account has the effect of reducing the value of that asset while the debit entry in the capital account reduces the owner's investment in the business by the value of the asset withdrawn.

When an owner makes fairly frequent withdrawals from the business for his private use, it is likely that an extra account will be introduced. This will be called the drawings account and it will be debited instead of the capital account. At the end of the financial year the total debit balance in this account can then be transferred into the capital account. An example will help to make this clear.

On the first day of March, June, September and December last year Judy Brooks withdrew £500 from the business bank account for private use. On 31 December she transferred the total amount withdrawn from drawings account to the capital account. The entries recording this were as follows.

Dr		Bank account		Cr
		1 March	Drawings	500
		1 June	Drawings	500
		1 Sept.	Drawings	500
		1 Dec.	Drawings	500

		Drawings account			
		£			
1 March	Bank	500	31 Dec.	Transferred to	
1 June	Bank	500		capital account	2,000
1 Sept.	Bank	500			
1 Dec.	Bank	500			
		2,000			2,000

		Capital account		
31 Dec.	Drawings	2,000		

Note the technique of transferring an amount from one account to another. We will meet this again in the next chapter. An entry is made on the smaller side of the account from which the transfer is to be made. This account is totalled and then closed. The double entry is completed by an entry on the other side of the account to which the transfer is being made. You are still following, therefore, the rules of double-entry book-keeping, because such a transfer requires one debit entry and one credit entry.

The end result is that the debit entry for £2,000 in the capital account reduces the owner's capital by that amount. The four credit entries in the bank account or cash book remove the £2,000 from the assets of the business. Using a drawings account does not hide the fact that assets taken out of a business by the owner for his private use reduce his capital investment in the business. It must not therefore be allowed to affect the calculation of profit.

Review

If you have understood this chapter you should be able to calculate Judy Brooks' profit for the year to 31 December 1981 from the information which follows. Take care – some information has been listed which is not needed. Provided you understand the difference between capital and revenue expenditure, and capital and revenue receipts, you should not find it too difficult.

Year ended 31 December 1981

	£
Sales revenue – meals and drinks	20,000
Cost of food and drinks sold	7,000
Purchase of equipment	2,000
Rent and rates	500
Depreciation on fixed assets	500
Loan from bank	1,000
Additional finance invested by owner	4,000
Insurances	200
Waiters' wages	4,000
Drawings	2,000
Gas and electricity	800

ANSWER

	£	£
Revenue receipts		
Sales revenue – meals and drinks		20,000
less *Revenue expenditure*		
Cost of meals and drinks sold	7,000	
Rent and rates	500	
Depreciation on fixed assets	500	
Insurance	200	
Waiters' wages	4,000	
Gas and electricity	800	13,000
Profit		7,000

The way in which you display the information does not matter for now. We will go into that in the next chapter. The important thing is that you obtained the correct answer and excluded from the calculation the information which was not relevant. Purchase of equipment is capital expenditure. Loan from the bank and additional finance invested by the owner are capital receipts. Drawings are regarded as a direct reduction of capital. Hence these items should not have entered into your calculation.

11 | Accounting for profit

The review question at the end of the last chapter tested your ability to calculate the profit of Judy Brooks' restaurant. In this chapter we are going to break down the concept of profit into two parts: gross profit and net profit. We will then consider how to prepare the accounts in which these profits will be measured. To do this we will need to return to the ledger account balances for information. Finally we will look once more at the balance sheet to see how making a profit (or loss) affects this statement of the financial affairs of a business.

First refer back to the answer to the last review question which you will find on page 152. You will see that the total amount of profit earned by Judy in 1981 was £7,000. This, in fact, is more correctly known as the net profit. Most businesses, however, do not calculate this figure by deducting total revenue expenditure from total sales revenue in one single calculation as we did. They introduce a preliminary stage in which gross profit is calculated.

Gross profit may be defined as the difference between the revenue earned from sales and the cost of the goods sold.

Self-check

Apply this definition to the information on page 152 and state Judy's gross profit for the year 1981.

ANSWER

1981	£
Revenue earned from sales of meals and drinks	20,000
Cost of goods (food and drinks) sold	7,000
Gross profit	13,000

As long as you understand the definition of gross profit you should not have found this difficult. Let's look at another example just in case. A friend of mine called Henry likes doing up motorcars in his spare time. He also enjoys wheeling and dealing. One day recently he bought an old Mini for £50 and was able to sell it within the week for £80. A very nice gross profit of £30 was made on that Mini.

On single deals like this it is not too difficult to state precisely the cost of the item sold and the revenue earned from selling it. When business becomes a little bigger, things become more complicated. Look at the following information for 1980 and you will see what I mean.

1 Jan.–31 Dec. Vehicles bought by Henry for £9,000.
1 Jan.–31 Dec. Revenue earned from sales £14,000.
1 Jan.   Henry's stock of vehicles: two Fords, cost price £500 each.
31 Dec.   Henry's stock of vehicles remaining: two Vauxhalls, cost price £750 each.

At first glance you might think that Henry's gross profit for 1980 was £5,000. This is calculated as the difference between revenue earned from sales (£14,000) and the cost of the vehicles bought (£9,000). Wait a minute, though, something is wrong here!

Self-check

Can you say why it is wrong to state that Henry's gross profit was £5,000?

ANSWER

Gross profit is the difference between the revenue earned from sales and the cost of goods sold. While it is correct to state that £14,000 revenue was earned from sales it is incorrect to deduct £9,000 from it. The total cost of the cars *bought* during the year was £9,000 but this is not the same as the cost of the cars actually sold. There are two reasons for this. First, some of the cars sold in 1980 had been bought the previous year and would have already been part of his stock at the beginning of the year. Second, some of the cars bought in 1980 had not been sold by the end of the year and form the closing stock on 31 December. Cost of goods sold is not, therefore, the same as the cost of goods bought.

The above explanation is important so read it through again carefully. To find how much gross profit Henry really made in 1980 we will need to work out the actual cost of the cars sold. A simple formula can be applied: *add the cost of the stock purchased to the opening stock at cost price.* This gives us the cost of stock *available* for sale. If we deduct from this the cost of the stock not sold – i.e. the closing stock at cost price – we are left with the actual cost of stock sold.

This can be seen more clearly in the following form:

- *opening stock at cost price:*
- add *cost of stock purchased during the year = cost of stock (or goods) available for sale;*
- deduct *closing stock at cost price = cost of stock sold.*

Self-check

Apply this formula to the information given about Henry's dealings and calculate his cost of stock sold for 1980. You will then be able to state accurately his gross profit for 1980.

ANSWER

	£
Opening stock at cost price	1,000
add Cost of stock purchased during year	9,000
Cost of stock available for sale	10,000
less Closing stock at cost price	1,500
Cost of stock sold 1980	8,500
Revenue earned from sales 1980	14,000
less Cost of stock sold 1980	8,500
Gross profit for 1980	5,500

Henry's gross profit of £5,500 seems very good – especially as it is earned from an interest which only occupies his spare time. However it is not the same as his true or **net profit**, which is the total revenue received from business operations less the total revenue expenditure incurred. So far we have only deducted one item of revenue expenditure – the actual cost of the cars sold. To calculate net profit you will have to deduct all the other items of revenue expenditure from the gross profit.

Self-check

Calculate Henry's net profit for 1980, taking into account the following additional information. (Note: make sure you use only those items which are relevant.)

Lubricants £100, machinery and equipment £800, tools £300, parts £700 and wages of part-time assistant £900.

ANSWER

	£	£
Gross profit 1980		5,500
less Wages	900	
Lubricants	100	
Parts	700	
	——	
		1,700
		——
Net profit for 1980		3,800

You should not have included expenditure on tools or machinery and equipment because these are examples of capital expenditure. As such they will benefit Henry's business for a number of years. If we knew how long they might last we could estimate how much depreciation on them should be deducted from this year's profits. In the absence of such information, no depreciation has been deducted.

The account in which profit is measured is called the **trading and profit and loss account**. The example below contains the information relating to Henry's business for 1980.

Trading and profit and loss account of Henry Reeve for the year ended 31 December 1980

	£	£
Sales		14,000
less *Cost of goods sold*		
Opening stock	1,000	
Purchases	9,000	
	10,000	
less Closing stock	1,500	
		8,500
Gross profit		5,500
less *Expenses*		
Wages	900	
Parts	700	
Lubricants	100	
		1,700
Net profit		3,800

Notes:
- The heading contains the name of the account, the name of the business or owner and the period for which profit is being measured.
- It is incorrect to date such an account 'as at 31 December' as you would a balance sheet, because it contains information relating to the measurement of profit over a particular time period. In the above example this period is a year, although of course there is nothing to prevent profit being measured for six months or any other time period.
- The section of the account in which gross profit is calculated is known as the trading section, while that in which net profit is measured is known as the profit and loss section. Sometimes these sections might appear as separate accounts, in which case gross profit is measured in the trading account and net profit in the profit and loss account.
- The style of the account shown above is one of a number that could be used. At one time the trading and profit and loss

account was prepared like a ledger account with debits (expenses) on the left and credits (incomes) on the right. This practice is less common today but examples can still be seen in certain textbooks. It is important that, whatever layout is used, the contents should be easily understood. Practice this by attempting the following.

Activity

Prepare a trading and profit and loss account from the following information relating to the business of Judy Brooks for the period from 1 Jan. 1982 to 30 June 1982.

	£
Sales of meals and drinks	16,000
Purchases of food and drinks	4,000
Returns outward	200
Stock of food and drink 1 Jan. 1982	400
Stock of food and drink 30 June 1982	600
Rent and rates	250
Depreciation on fixed assets	250
Insurance	100
Waiters' wages	3,000
Gas and electricity	500

ANSWER

Trading and profit and loss account of Judy Brooks for the six months ended 30 June 1982

	£	£	£
Sales			16,000
less *Cost of goods sold*			
Opening stock		400	
Purchases	4,000		
less Returns outward	200		
Net purchases		3,800	
		4,200	
less Closing stock		600	
			3,600
Gross profit			12,400

less *Expenses*

Waiters' wages	3,000	
Rent and rates	250	
Depreciation on fixed assets	250	
Insurance	100	
Gas and electricity	500	
		4,100
Net profit		8,300

The item that may have caused most problems is returns outward, which is otherwise known as purchases returns. These are goods which have been bought but which, for some reason, are then returned to the supplier. We dealt with the relevant ledger entries on page 55.

Clearly, any purchases to be included in the cost of goods sold figure must be available for sale. Those which are returned before being sold must therefore be deducted from the purchases figure to arrive at true or net purchases.

We must now look back to the ledger and see what happens to the accounts which contain the items appearing in the trading and profit and loss account. Assume that, before Judy's trading and profit and loss account was prepared, the trial balance shown opposite was extracted from her ledger.

The balances in the accounts which are needed to calculate profit will be transferred to the trading and profit and loss account. The process of transferring an amount from one account to another was demonstrated in the last chapter when drawings were transferred from the drawings account to the capital account. I will remind you how to do it by showing the transfer of sales.

Trial balance of Judy Brooks as at 30 June 1982

Account	£ dr	£ cr
Capital (1 Jan. 1982)		3,300
Equipment	4,000	
Furniture and fittings	6,000	
China, linen and cutlery	800	
Stock (1 Jan. 1982)	400	
Debtors	100	
Cash at bank	400	
Trade creditors		300
Sales		16,000
Purchases	4,000	
Returns outward		200
Waiters' wages	3,000	
Rent and rates	250	
Depreciation on fixed assets	250	
Insurance	100	
Gas and electricity	500	
	19,800	19,800

Dr			Sales account		Cr
1982		£	*1982*		£
30 June	Transferred to		31 Jan.	Cash	2,000
	trading a/c	16,000	28 Feb.	Cash	3,000
			31 Mar.	Cash	4,000
			30 Apr.	Cash	2,000
			31 May	Cash	3,000
			30 June	Cash	2,000
		16,000			16,000

Whatever the total, this amount is placed on the smaller side with the date of transfer and a suitable description. The account is then totalled and totals are underlined. The account is thus temporarily closed and will be opened again when the first sales are recorded in the next financial period.

Self-check

Show the transfer of purchases to Judy's trading account.
You may assume that the purchases were made as follows:
Jan. – May £600 each month by cheque and June £1,000 on
credit.

ANSWER

Dr			Purchases account		Cr
1982		£	*1982*		£
31 Jan.	Bank	600	30 June	Transferred to	
28 Feb.	Bank	600		trading a/c	4,000
31 Mar.	Bank	600			
30 Apr.	Bank	600			
31 May	Bank	600			
30 June	Creditors	1,000			
		4,000			4,000

The only account in which complications arise is the stock
account. This is because two stock figures are needed in the
trading account while at any one time there will be only one
balance for stock shown in the trial balance. It is important to
realise that, unless told otherwise, the stock balance in the trial
balance will be the opening stock for the period. Stock will be
valued at the end of the period and this figure will be entered in
both the trading account and the stock account. Here is how the
stock account will appear after the trading and profit and loss
account has been prepared.

Dr			Stock account		Cr
		£			£
1 Jan.	Balance b/d	400	30 June	Transferred to	400
				trading a/c	
30 June	Trading a/c	600			

Do not be confused by the two entries dated 30 June. Although the credit entry is dated 30 June it is, in fact, the opening stock of 1 Jan. which is being transferred to the trading account on 30 June. The closing stock at 30 June is shown by the debit entry for £600. The description 'trading account' is used because that is where the other double entry can be found. As mentioned earlier, the practice of actually showing the trading and profit and loss account as a ledger account with two distinct sides has been largely discontinued. Those readers interested in the theory of double-entry book-keeping might like to see how the trading section would have been shown. The one below makes use of the same figures for Judy Brooks as does the one on page 159.

Trading account of Judy Brooks for six months ended 30 June 1982

	£		£
Opening stock	400	Sales	16,000
Purchases	4,000	Returns outward	200
Balance (gross profit)	12,400	Closing stock	600
	16,800		16,800

The entries for opening stock, purchases, sales and returns outward appear on the same side as they would have done in their individual accounts. The credit entry for closing stock is the entry corresponding to the debit made in the stock account after the stocktaking at the end of the year. The balance of the account is the gross profit. This figure is exactly the same as arrived at earlier. I am sure you will agree that, while this method gives the same answer, the process of obtaining it is nothing like as clear.

We have looked at the process by which some ledger accounts balances are transferred to the trading and profit and loss account. Now we need to consider what happens to those balances which remain in the accounts after the profit has been calculated.

Self-check

Look back to the trial balance on page 161 and identify those accounts which will still have balances in them because they will *not* have been transferred to the trading and profit and loss account.

ANSWER

The following accounts will still have balances: capital, equipment, furniture and fittings, china, linen and cutlery, debtors, trade creditors, cash at bank and stock (for the closing balance). Can you see what they all have in common? A glance back to page 18 may remind you. They are all balance sheet items.

Having closed all the accounts involving revenue receipts and revenue expenditure, we are left only with balances in the accounts for assets and sources of finance. The balances in these accounts can now be placed in a balance sheet showing the position of Judy's business at the end of the financial period. Before we do this, there is one final double entry to be made. The net profit of £8,300 belongs to the owner. The entry for this amount in the profit and loss account must be accompanied by another in the account of the owner, which is, of course, the capital account.

Dr		Capital account			Cr
		£			£
30 June	Balance c/d	11,600	1 Jan.	Balance b/d	3,300
			30 June	Net profit	8,300
					11,600
		11,600	1 July	Balance b/d	11,600

The credit entry for net profit increases Judy's capital. If a loss has been made a debit entry would be needed in the capital account to reduce her capital balance.

When all the remaining accounts are balanced at the end of June, the balance sheet will look like this:

Balance sheet of Judy Brooks as at 30 June 1982

	£	£		£	£
Owners' capital	3,300		*Fixed assets*		
			Furniture and		
			fittings	6,000	
add Net profit	8,300		Equipment	4,000	
		11,600	China, etc.	800	
					10,800
Current liabilities			*Current assets*		
Trade creditors		300	Stock	600	
			Debtors	100	
			Cash at bank	400	
					1,100
		11,900			11,900

As the balance sheet has not appeared since very early in the book, you may have to remind yourself of its presentation by looking back to Chapter 2. You might think that the owners' capital could have been shown by one figure for £11,600. This is, after all, the balance in the capital account and the balance sheet is a collection of all the balances remaining in the accounts after preparation of the trading and profit and loss account. It is normal practice, however, to show all the information in the capital account again in the form of a sum in the balance sheet. Thus if Judy had drawn any assets for her private use we would also show this, as it is a reduction of her capital.

The above balance sheet is known as a horizontal balance sheet because the sources of finance are arranged to the side of the assets. Nowadays many businesses make use of a vertical presentation in which the finance appears beneath the assets. This matter of presentation is developed in *Practical Accounts 2* in the Pan Breakthrough series.

Before you proceed to answer a question which will serve to review the contents of this chapter, a few points ought to be made about some accounts which often cause confusion (and are frequently included in examination questions, therefore).

Carriage inwards and carriage outwards

These are both expenses and therefore appear as debit balances in their ledger accounts. The first is the expense of paying for the transport of goods which have been bought for resale. The second describes the expense of transporting goods sold to the customers. They are treated slightly differently, however, in the trading and profit and loss account. Carriage inwards is added to the purchases in the trading section while carriage outwards is listed with all the other expenses in the profit and loss account.

Discounts allowed and discounts received

Discounts allowed to debtors for prompt payment are shown as an expense in the profit and loss section. Discounts received from creditors are shown as income in the profit and loss account along with any other income such as rent received. Such incomes are usually positioned immediately below the gross profit.

It could be argued that, as discount allowed is an expense arising from the sale of goods, it should be shown in the trading section. Similarly it might be argued that discounts received arise from purchases and should be shown as income in the trading section. In practice this is not normally done.

Self-check

Which of the following items appears in the trading section of the trading and profit and loss account: carriage inwards, carriage outwards, discount received, discount allowed?

ANSWER

Carriage inwards. Reread the last two sections if you failed to answer correctly.

The trading and profit and loss account and the balance sheet are often known as the final accounts because they are drawn up at the end of the financial year. Technically the balance sheet is not an account but a financial statement. You can normally assume, however, that when you are asked to prepare final accounts, a balance sheet is to be prepared as well.

The following question tests your ability to apply what has

been dealt with in this chapter. You may not find it easy, but careful consideration of the solution, together with reference back to the text, should enable you to understand it fully.

Review

The following trial balance was extracted from the ledger of Frank Holden, a retailer. Prepare his trading and profit and loss account for the year ended 31 August 1981 and a balance sheet as at that date.

	£ dr	£ cr
Capital (1 Sept. 1980)		30,400
Cash	150	
Bank	1,700	
Stock (1 Sept. 1980)	8,000	
Purchases and purchases returns	69,000	1,200
Sales and sales returns	260	96,400
Carriage inwards	940	
Carriage outwards	320	
Discount allowed and received	920	1,380
Wages	8,000	
Depreciation on fixed assets	1,000	
Drawings	9,000	
Rent received		630
Premises	25,000	
Fixtures and fittings	5,000	
Motor vehicles	1,500	
Trade debtors and creditors	480	3,620
Rates	520	
Insurance	490	
Heating and lighting	800	
Miscellaneous expenses	550	
	133,630	133,630

Note:

● Stock on 31 August 1981 was valued at £12,000.

● Some of the balances have been combined together, for example trade debtors and creditors. Your knowledge of balances in the ledger should enable you to decide which figure refers to which item.

ANSWER

Trading and profit and loss account of Frank Holden for the year ended
31 August 1981

	£	£	£
Sales		96,400	
less Sales returns		260	
Net turnover			96,140
less *Cost of goods sold*			
Opening stock		8,000	
Purchases	69,000		
less Purchases returns	1,200		
	67,800		
Carriage inwards	940		
Net purchases		68,740	
		76,740	
less Closing stock		12,000	
			64,740
Gross profit			31,400
Discount received			1,380
Rent received			630
Total revenue			33,410
less *Expenses*			
Wages		8,000	
Insurance		490	
Heating and lighting		800	
Rates		520	
Depreciation		1,000	
Carriage outwards		320	
Discount allowed		920	
Miscellaneous		550	12,600
Net profit			20,810

Balance sheet of Frank Holden as at 31 August 1981

	£	£		£	£
Owner's capital	30,400		*Fixed assets*		
add Net profit	20,810		Premises	25,000	
			Fixtures and		
	51,210		fittings	5,000	
less Drawings	9,000		Motor vehicle	1,500	
		42,210			31,500
Current liabilities			*Current assets*		
Trade creditors		3,620	Stock	12,000	
			Debtors	480	
			Bank	1,700	
			Cash	150	
					14,330
		45,830			45,830

12 | Prepayments and accruals

We have now covered the whole process involved in keeping a set of financial accounts – from opening a ledger and keeping track of transactions there and in the journals to preparing the final accounts at the end of the period. In the remaining chapters we will consider the reasons why certain adjustments have to be made to the information recorded in our books. We will also see how these adjustments can be made. In addition I will take the opportunity of giving you some additional practice preparing the final accounts. This chapter will cover the adjustments which arise because payments and receipts of money do not always occur in the financial period to which the expenditure or income relates.

Expenses prepaid

Consider the following facts about a new business which was established on 1 January 1981 and therefore has a financial year which is the same as the calendar year.

All insurances were negotiated with a broker and the premiums payable amounted to £400 per annum. The business negotiated terms which allowed this amount to be paid in four quarterly instalments of £100 each. These instalments were due on the first day of January, April, July and October.

Self-check

Assuming that the instalments were paid by cheque on the dates due, show the insurance account as it would have appeared after preparation of the final accounts for the year.

ANSWER

Dr			Insurance account			Cr
1981			£	1981		£
1 Jan.	Bank		100	31 Dec. Transferred to profit		
1 Apr.	Bank		100	and loss account		400
1 July	Bank		100			
1 Oct.	Bank		100			
			———			———
			400			400

This should not have caused you any difficulty as it simply involved revision of the work done earlier. Insurance is an expense and, as such, debit entries are used to record its payment in the insurance account. The credit entries will appear in the bank column of the cash book.

Suppose, however, that in 1982 the insurance account looked like this:

Dr		Insurance account	Cr
1982		£	
1 Jan.	Bank	100	
1 Apr.	Bank	100	
1 July	Bank	100	
1 Oct.	Bank	100	
20 Dec.	Bank	100	

You might think that the cost of insurance for this firm had increased from £400 per annum to £500 per annum. While that might be true, it is not the case here. The insurance premiums remained at £400 per annum. What, then, do you think explains the extra £100 recorded? The only logical answer is that the payment of £100 on 20 December 1982 was made early. It was really the amount due on 1 January 1983. This is an example of a prepaid expense, which is what this section of the chapter is about. A prepaid expense is one which is paid in the period prior to the one in which it is due.

You might wonder whether or not it is correct to record such a payment when it is made on 20 December 1982. After all, it is an amount which belongs to 1983, and it might be argued that it should not be recorded until that year has begun. It is in fact correct to record it on the date it was paid and thus the account is in perfect order, as it stands.

This does cause a problem, however. How much should be transferred to the profit and loss account of 1982 as the expense of insurance? The answer is £400, which is the true expense for 1982. The additional £100 is really an expense which relates to 1983 and will be included in that year's profit and loss account. The principle on which this is based is that costs or expenses should be counted when they are incurred and not when they are paid. Thus £400 is counted as the expense of insurance for 1982. The additional £100 will count as part of the insurance for 1983.

There remains the technique of transferring to the profit and loss account the correct amount of £400. This is what the insurance account will look like when it has been done:

Dr			Insurance a/c		Cr
1982		£	*1982*		£
1 Jan.	Bank	100	31 Dec. Transferred to profit		
1 Apr.	Bank	100	and loss account		400
1 July	Bank	100	31 Dec. Balance prepaid c/d		100
1 Oct.	Bank	100			
20 Dec.	Bank	100			
		500			500
1983					
1 Jan.	Balance prepaid b/d	100			

As you can see, the problem has been overcome by bringing down the amount prepaid as a balance for the start of the next financial year. This procedure is quite correct because, after preparation of the trading and profit and loss account, all ledger accounts having balances within them should be balanced. I wonder if you can remember what happens to all accounts which contain balances. If you thought 'they appear in the statement known as the balance sheet', well done! Perhaps you can even work out where in the balance sheet the £100 insurance should appear. It is in fact an asset, one clue being that it is brought down as a debit balance. You should be able to recognise the logic of this as it is an asset to the firm in that it will receive insurance in 1983 for which payment has already been made in 1982. The fact that this benefit relates to such a short time period means that it is a current asset and not a fixed asset. The relevant balance sheet entry will look like this:

Balance sheet as at 31 Dec. 1982

	£
Current assets	
Stock	—
Debtors	—
Bank	—
Prepaid insurance	100

Some textbooks advise placing prepayments with, or next to, the debtors. This is acceptable as logically the benefit of insurance which is to be received is owed by the insurance company to the firm which has paid for it in advance. Others prefer to place it last on the grounds that it is more liquid than cash in that the money has already been spent. I leave the choice to you but would stress the value of consistency. Once you have decided where you are going to show prepaid expenses in the balance sheet, stick to it.

Self-check

Harry Wilson's financial year ends on 30 June. He rents his premises at £200 per quarter which is payable on 1 July, 1 October, 1 January and 1 April. In the year ended 30 June 1981, which was his first year of trading, he made the following payments by cheque: 1 July 1980, £200; 3 October 1980, £200; 1 January 1981, £200; 2 April 1981, £200; 4 June 1981, £200.

Write up Harry's ledger account for rent and show all entries relevant to the final accounts at the end of the year. Be especially careful with the dates. It is never as easy when the financial year differs from the calendar year.

ANSWER

Dr			Rent account		Cr
1980		£	*1981*		£
1 July	Bank	200	30 June	Transferred to profit	
3 Oct.	Bank	200		and loss account	800
			30 June	Balance prepaid c/d	200
1981					
1 Jan.	Bank	200			
2 Apr.	Bank	200			
4 June	Bank	200			
		1,000			1,000
1 July	Balance prepaid b/d	200			

Profit and loss account of Harry Wilson for the year ended 30 June 1981

	£
Expenses	
Rent	800

Balance sheet of Harry Wilson as at 30 June 1981

	£
Current assets	
Prepaid rent	200

As you were told that the premiums amounted to £200 per quarter, and there are four quarters in a year, it is clear that £800 must be the true expense of rent incurred in the year ending 30 June 1981. The additional £200 must therefore relate to the next financial year and be brought forward as a debit balance in the rent account. It thus represents an asset to Harry at the end of June 1981. In the first quarter of his next financial year he will enjoy the use of premises for which he has already paid.

In both the example I gave you and the self-check you knew the true cost of the expense for the year. Sometimes, however, you are told how much has been paid for an expense and how much of that is a prepayment. You then have to calculate the correct amount to be transferred to the profit and loss account. This often happens in an examination when you are given a trial balance entry and told by how much it should be adjusted. For example, the following item appeared in Harry's trial balance at 30 June 1981.

A/cs	dr	cr
Rates	350	

You are then told that, of the rates, £50 has been paid in advance for the year ending 30 June 1982. Deducting this from the amount paid gives you the true value of rates for the year ended 30 June 1981, that is, £300. The accounts would look like this:

Dr			Rates account		Cr
1980/1		£	*1981*		£
—	Bank	350	30 June	Profit and loss a/c	300
			30 June	Balance prepaid c/d	50
		350			350
1981					
1 July	Balance prepaid b/d	50			

Profit and loss account of Harry Wilson, year ended 30 June 1981

	£
Expenses	
Rates	300

Balance sheet of Harry Wilson as at 30 June 1981

	Current assets	
	Prepaid rates	50

Self-check

The following item appeared in the trial balance of a business at 31 October 1981.

A/cs	dr	cr
Rent	944	

You are told that £68 of the rent has been paid in advance for the next financial year.

Show the rent account balanced at 31 October and the relevant entries in the final accounts.

ANSWER

Dr			Rent account		Cr
1980/81		£	*1981*		£
—	Bank	944	31 Oct.	Profit and loss a/c	876
			31 Oct.	Balance prepaid c/d	68
		944			944
1981					
1 Nov.	Balance prepaid b/d	68			

Profit and loss account, year ended 31 October 1981

	£
Expenses	
Rent	876

Balance sheet as at 31 October 1981

	£
Current assets	
Prepaid rent	68

In examination questions you are frequently asked only to prepare the final accounts. If this is the case you may still decide to prepare a ledger account for any trial balance items that need adjustments. It might help you to get the answer right but it is not essential. You can do the adjustment arithmetically and, if you wish, show it within the profit and loss account. For example the entry in the profit and loss account of the last self-check could have been shown like this:

	£	£
Expenses		
Rent	944	
less Prepayment	68	
		876

Self-check

Complete the following table in which **a** has been done for you.

	Trial balance 31.12.1980		Prepaid at 31.12.1980	Profit and loss a/c yr ended 31.12.1980	Current asset in balance sheet as at 31.12.1980
A/c		dr	£	£	£
a Rent		900	100	800	100 prepaid rent
b Rates		750	150		
c Insurance		620		480	
d Salaries			640	4,320	
e Fuel				1,600	300 prepaid fuel
f Wages		490			120 prepaid wages

ANSWER

b Profit and loss a/c £600, current asset £150 rates prepaid.

c Prepaid at 31.12.1980 £140, current asset £140 insurance prepaid.

d Trial balance £4,960, current asset £640 salaries prepaid.

e Trial balance £1,900, prepaid at 31.12.1980 £300.

f Prepaid at 31.12.1980 £120, profit and loss a/c £370.

Expenses accrued

The word 'accrued' here means 'owing' or 'outstanding'. Thus an accrued expense is one which is owing for a financial period but which is not paid until a subsequent period.

For example, suppose that a business rents property for £1,200 per annum and that this sum is payable in four instalments on the first day of January, April, July and October. In 1980 the rent account looked like this when the firm's financial year ended on 31 December:

Dr		Rent account	Cr
1980		£	
1 Jan.	Bank	300	
1 April	Bank	300	
1 Sept.	Bank	300	

Self-check

Would it be correct to transfer the £900 contained in this account to the profit and loss account as the total expense of rent for the year ended 31 December 1980?

ANSWER

No. This would not be in agreement with the principle we set out earlier in this chapter. This states that costs or expenses should be counted when they are incurred and not when they are paid. The cost incurred of renting premises in 1980 is £1,200. This amount, and not the amount paid, is the true expense of rent for 1980 and must be shown therefore in the profit and loss account.

In order to transfer the correct amount to the profit and loss account the amount outstanding is inserted on the debit side as a balance accrued to carry down at the end of the year. It is then possible to transfer £1,200 to the profit and loss account. This amount is made up of £900 actually paid and £300 owing. Of course, it is necessary that any balance carried down is then brought down to the other side of the account. The balance is brought down to the credit side which indicates that it is a liability at the end of the year. As such it will appear in the balance sheet and, because it is likely that payment will have to be made very soon indeed, it will be placed next to the creditors in the current liabilities.

When completed, the rent account and the relevant entries in the final accounts will look like this:

Dr			Rent account		Cr
1980		£	*1980*		£
1 Jan.	Bank	300	31 Dec.	Profit and loss	1,200
1 Apr.	Bank	300			
1 Sept.	Bank	300			
31 Dec.	Balance accrued c/d	300			
		1,200			1,200
			1981		
			1 Jan.	Balance accrued b/d	300

Profit and loss account, year ended 31 Dec. 1980

	£
Expenses	
Rent	1,200

Balance sheet as at 31 Dec. 1980

	£
Current liabilities	
Accrued rent	300

Self-check

The trial balance of a firm whose financial year ends on 31 March 1981 contains the following item.

A/cs	£ dr	£ cr
Wages	30,000	

Because the weekly wages were last made up on 26 March the amount of £350 has accrued by 31 March. Make the necessary adjustments to the wages account and show the relevant entries in the final accounts for the year ended 31 March 1981.

ANSWER

Dr			Wages account		Cr
1980/81		£	*1981*		£
	Cash book	30,000	31 Mar.	Profit and	
31 Mar.	Balance accrued			loss a/c	30,350
	c/d	350			
		30,350			
					30,350
			1 April	Balance accrued	
				b/d	30,350

Profit and loss account year ended 31 March 1981

	£
Expenses	
Wages	30,350

Balance sheet as at 31 March 1981

	£
Current liabilities	
Accrued wages	350

Many examination questions require only the final accounts to be shown. While you may decide to complete the ledger account adjustment as an aid to obtaining the correct answer, it is not absolutely necessary. The adjustment could be shown in the profit and loss account like this:

Profit and loss account year ended 31 March 1981

	£	£
Expenses		
Wages	30,000	
add Accrual	350	
		30,350

The key point to keep in mind when deciding how the amount of an expense is to be shown in the profit and loss account is the date it is incurred. If the expense refers to, say, 1980, it must be included in that year's profit and loss account. If the full amount has not been paid in 1980 then the expense account must be adjusted to show the true expense for the period. Remember, however, to include any such adjustment for an expense outstanding in the balance sheet under the heading of current liabilities.

Self-check

As a final check on your understanding of accruals, complete the following table, in which **a** has been done for you.

Trial balance 31.12.1981 A/c dr	Accrued at 31.12.1981 £	Profit and loss a/c yr ended 31.12.1981 £	Current liability in balance sheet as at 31.12.1981 £
a Rent 600	200	800	200 accrued rent
b Rates 400	300		
c Insurance 750		820	
d Wages	100	800	
e Salaries		900	300 accrued salary
f Fuel 420			90 accrued fuel

ANSWER

b Profit and loss a/c £700, current liability £300 rates accrued.
c Accrued at 31.12 £70, current liability £70 insurance accrued.
d Trial balance £700, current liability £100 wages accrued.
e Trial balance £600, accrued at 31.12 £300.
f Accrued at 31.12 £90, profit and loss a/c £510.

Income prepaid

The rule to follow when allocating income to the correct accounting period is the same as the one we applied to costs. Income or revenue is counted when goods are sold or services provided, not when the money is received. We have dealt already with the sale of goods on credit. The amount of the sale is credited to the sales account and a debit entry is made in the account of the customer who is a debtor. The total sales will be transferred to the trading account at the end of the period whether or not the customer has paid for them. Similarly all other income must be shown in its correct period.

For example, suppose a restaurant owner rents out the flat above his business to earn extra profit. He charges £100 per month and his financial year ends on 31 December. In the year ended 31 December 1980 the tenant paid the amounts due on the first of each month and in December he made an additional payment of £100 for January 1981. The rent received account will have been credited with a total of £1,300 and in the trial balance it will look like this:

	£ dr	£ cr
Rent received		1,300

It would be wrong, however, to show the whole amount in the profit and loss account as income for the year ended 31 December 1980. Clearly £100 is income for 1981. This amount must therefore be deducted from the £1,300 to show the correct income relating to 1980 as £1,200. The ledger account and final accounts entries will look like this:

Dr			Rent received account			Cr
1980		£	*1980*			£
31 Dec.	Profit and loss a/c	1,200	1 Jan. – 31 Dec.	Bank (total)		1,300
31 Dec.	Balance prepaid c/d	100				
		1,300				1,300
			1981			
			1 Jan.	Balance prepaid b/d		100

Profit and loss account year ended 31 Dec. 1980

	£
Gross profit	—
Rent received	1,200

Balance sheet as at 31 Dec. 1980

	£
Current liabilities	
Rent received in advance	100

As an income the £1,200 rent received is added to the gross profit. The £100 received in advance represents a liability to the owner of the restaurant. He owes this sum, or rather the use of the flat which is worth this amount, to his tenant. It therefore appears in the balance sheet as a current liability. Note that this is the exact opposite to an expense prepaid which counts as a current asset in the balance sheet.

Self-check

Show the final accounts' entries relating to the following.

A hotel allows local firms to advertise in the foyer for which it makes a charge. During the year ended 30 June 1980 it had received £250 income for this. However, one firm has paid £20 in June for an advertisement to be displayed in July 1980.

ANSWER

Profit and loss account year ended 30 June 1980

	£	£
Advertising received	250	
less Prepayment	20	230

Balance sheet as at 30 June 1980

	£
Current liabilities	
Advertising received in advance	20

Income accrued

Sometimes a business will not have received all the income to which it is entitled by the end of its financial year. When this happens, the amount owing or accrued must be added to what has been received to show the true income for the year. For example a retailer rents part of his store room to another firm and charges £50 per month. On 31 December 1980, when his financial year ends, only eleven months' rent has been received. The rent received account will appear in the trial balance like this:

	£ dr	£ cr
Rent received		550

It is necessary to adjust the rent received account so that the correct amount of £600 can be transferred to the profit and loss account. The ledger account and the final accounts' entries will look like this:

Dr		Rent received account			Cr
1980		£	*1980*		£
31 Dec.	Profit and loss a/c	600	1 Jan. – 31 Dec. Bank		
				(total)	550
			31 Dec. Balance accrued		
				c/d	50
		———			———
		600			600
		———			———
1981					
1 Jan.	Balance accrued				
	b/d	50			

Profit and loss account, year ended 31 Dec. 1980

Gross profit	—
Rent received	600

Balance sheet as at 31 Dec. 1980

	£
Current assets	
Rent due	50

The £50 due from the tenant is a debt which the retailer will count as a current asset. In practice it will probably be included with sundry debtors.

Self-check

Show the entries in the final accounts relating to the following.

In the year ended 31 October 1980 a hotel received £160 for allowing firms to advertise in its reception area. One firm, however, had not paid a bill of £40 for an advertisement displayed in September.

ANSWER

Profit and loss account, year ended 31 Oct. 1980

	£	£
Advertising received	160	
add Accrual	40	
		200

Balance sheet as at 31 Oct. 1980

	£
Current assets	
Advertising due	40

Review

The following question will test your understanding of this chapter and provide practice in preparing final accounts.

Trial balance of the White Hart Hotel as at 31 October 1981

	£	£
Capital		85,800
Stocks (1 Nov. 1980)	2,250	
Loan from Busifinance		15,000
Leasehold premises	97,500	
Furniture and equipment	22,500	
Debtors	900	
Creditors		750
Advertising and insurance	1,905	
Salaries and wages	16,500	
Rates	1,350	
Discount received		105
Discount allowed	300	
Purchases	37,500	
Rent received		1,800
Bank	1,500	
Heat and light	825	
Sundry expenses	675	
Cash	150	
Sales		84,000
Drawings	3,600	
	187,455	187,455

Taking into account the following matters, prepare a trading and profit and loss account for the year ended 31 October 1981 and a balance sheet at that date.

a Stocks at 31 October 1981 were valued at £3,000.
b Wages outstanding amounted to £200 on 31 October 1981.
c Insurance paid in advance on 31 October 1981 was £30.
d The loan from Busifinance was made on 31 July at an agreed interest of 12% per annum. This had not been paid.
e The rent received of £1,800 included £200 in advance for November 1981.

If you find this exercise difficult, don't be alarmed. It does contain a great deal of information. It is probable that any errors you made will have included the adjustments as these are the difficult parts. Look carefully at the items in the profit and loss account and use your reasoning powers to satisfy yourself that each one is correct. Very often students forget that an adjustment will also require an entry in the balance sheet and this will result in the totals of this statement not agreeing. It is worth remembering that any adjustment to be made to items contained in a trial balance will affect both profit and loss account *and* balance sheet. When a balance sheet does not agree, therefore, the first thing to do in an exercise like the one above is to check that you have accounted for each adjustment in both statements.

ANSWER

Trading and profit and loss account of the White Hart Hotel for the year ended 31 October 1981

	£	£	£
Sales			84,000
less *Cost of sales*			
Opening stocks		2,250	
Purchases		37,500	
		39,750	
less Closing stocks		3,000	
			36,750
Gross profit			47,250
Discounts received			105
Rent received		1,800	
less Prepayment		200	
			1,600
			48,955
less *Expenses*			
Salaries and wages	16,500		
add Wages accrued	200		
		16,700	
Advertising and insurance	1,905		
less Insurance prepaid	30		
		1,875	
Interest on loan accrued		450	
Rates		1,350	
Discount allowed		300	
Heat and light		825	
Sundry expenses		675	
			22,175
Net profit			26,780

Balance sheet of the White Hart Hotel as at 31 October 1981

	£	£		£	£
Capital	85,800		*Fixed assets*		
add Net profit	26,780		Leasehold		
			premises	97,500	
	112,580		Furniture and		
less Drawings	3,600		equipment	22,500	
		108,980			120,000
Long-term liabilities			*Current assets*		
Loan		15,000	Stocks	3,000	
			Debtors	900	
Current liabilities			Prepaid		
Creditors	750		insurance	30	
Wages accrued	200		Bank	1,500	
Interest accrued	450		Cash	150	
Rent received in					
advance	200	1,600			5,580
		125,580			125,580

13 | Providing for bad debts

In this chapter we are going to look at an adjustment involving debtors. It will enable the true amount of bad debts for a period to be included in that period's profit and loss account. In addition the asset 'debtors' will be shown at its proper value in the balance sheet. There are two methods of book-keeping that can be used. Both of these will be illustrated because examiners frequently specify by which method they require a question to be answered. When you have mastered the process of providing for bad debts and recording the recovery of debts previously written off as bad, there will be an opportunity to gain extra practice in the preparation of final accounts.

You are advised to reread the section on bad debts in Chapter 5 before you begin this chapter.

Self-check

Fill in the blanks:

1 Bad debts are the _____ incurred when debtors fail to pay their debts.
2 In the balance sheet, debtors appear as an _____ because it is assumed that anyone to whom credit has been allowed will pay what they owe.
3 Once it is known that a debt is never going to be collected this fact must be shown in the accounts. If it were not, then the accounts would not be giving a _____ _____ of the assets of the business.
4 It is accepted that _____ _____ a bad debt is an occasional and inevitable part of allowing credit to others.

ANSWERS

1 Expense (or cost or loss), **2** asset, **3** fair (or true) picture, **4** writing off. If you got them all right, either you have a very good memory or you took the advice above and reread the section in Chapter 5. If you didn't get them right, read that section now.

We are going to learn about providing for bad debts by following a business which started on 1 January 1980. That was the day when A. Rowe began trading as a wholesaler.

The thought of his customers failing to pay their debts did not occur to him at first. He soon learnt! By the end of his first financial year he had written off £300 worth of bad debts. The bad debts account appeared like this after the expense had been transferred to the profit and loss account:

Dr			Bad debts account		Cr
1980		£	*1980*		£
1 Jan. – 31 Dec.	Sundry		31 Dec.	Transferred to profit	
	debtors	300		and loss account	300
		300			300

At the same time the debit balance in his sundry debtors' account showed that customers owed him £4,000.

	Sundry debtors account	
1980	£	
31 Dec. Balance	4,000	

Two thoughts occurred to him: first, that it was likely that some of this £4,000 would probably not be paid. In other words it included some debts that would prove to be bad. The figure in the profit and loss account was thus likely to be an understatement of the *real* amount of bad debts for the year. Second, if he showed the £4,000 in the balance sheet at 31 December as an asset, he would be overstating the value of this asset. He decided to take the advice of a friendly accountant and created a provision for bad debts. This was done in three steps and helped to overcome the problems mentioned above.

- He estimated the amount of likely bad debts. In this case Rowe decided £200 was about the right amount to allow for.
- This amount was entered in the profit and loss account as an expense, thus reducing the net profit by £200. The profit and loss account now included two amounts as an expense for bad debts: the actual bad debts written off for the year and an estimate of those likely to be written off – the provision.

Profit and loss account, year ended 31 December 1980

	£
Expenses	
Bad debts	300
Provision for bad debts	200

- The double entry corresponding to this entry in the profit and loss account for estimated bad debts was made in a provision for bad debts account thus:

Dr	Provision for bad debts account	Cr
	1980	£
	31 Dec. Profit and loss account	200

This is a credit balance at the end of the year and therefore appears in the balance sheet. As a credit balance it is technically a source of finance, i.e. finance taken out of profits to be used for writing off bad debts when they occur. Instead of showing this with the other finance, however, it is usual practice to show it as a deduction from the asset debtors.

Balance sheet of A. Rowe as at 31 Dec. 1980

	£
Current assets	
Debtors	4,000
less Provision, bad debts	200
	3,800

Thus the balance sheet now shows debtors at a more realistic valuation. The question arises as to how much should be provided for bad debts. Greatest accuracy would be achieved if all the debts in the accounts were analysed at the end of the year to decide which ones were most likely to prove uncollectable. In practice those debts which have been due longest will probably be the most suspect. This, however, is a time-consuming process and it is much simpler to allow a certain percentage for probable bad debts, as we did in the example above. Experience will show us how accurate the figure is and, if necessary, it can be adjusted upwards or downwards.

Self-check

Simon Robinson began trading as a retailer on 1 January 1980. By the end of his first year of trading he had written off a total of £140 worth of debts as irrecoverable. On 31 December 1980 his debts were valued in the books at £2,500. He decided to create a provision for bad debts which would allow for 5% of that amount to be irrecoverable. Show the bad debts account, provision for bad debts account and relevant entries in his final accounts.

ANSWER

Dr				Bad debts account			Cr
1980			£	*1980*			£
1 Jan. – 31 Dec.	Sundry debtors		140	31 Dec.	Transferred to profit and loss account		140

			Provision for bad debts account			
1980			£	*1980*			£
				31 Dec.	Profit and loss account		125
31 Dec.	Balance c/d		125				
				1981			
				1 Jan.	Balance b/d		125

Profit and loss account of Simon Robinson, year ended 31 Dec. 1980

	£
Expenses	
Bad debts	140
Provision for bad debts	125

Balance sheet of Simon Robinson as at 31 December 1980

	£
Current assets	
Debtors	2,500
less Provision for bad debts	125
	2,375

It is very important when dealing with this matter to read the instructions of a question carefully. Sometimes you may be asked to write off the actual bad debts *before* creating a provision based on the figure remaining in the debtors' account. In this self-check the actual bad debts had already been written off. The provision therefore had to be based on the £2,500 actually in the account on 31 December.

Note that on both the bad debts account and the provision for bad debts account there is an entry relating to the profit and loss account. However, there is a difference. The entry in the bad debts account is made to transfer that debit balance to the profit and loss account. The entry in the provision account is a credit entry made to correspond to the debit entry in the profit and loss account which is made first. In effect £125 of finance is being taken from the profits and specifically earmarked to cover future bad debts. It is very important that you realise that this adjustment does not actually involve the movement of any cash.

Once a provision for bad debts has been created there are two methods by which you can proceed:

1 All entries relating to bad debts from now on can be made in the provision account.
2 Separate accounts are maintained for actual bad debts and the provision for bad debts.

We will consider each in turn using the business of A. Rowe as an illustration.

Method 1 Remind yourself of the position of A. Rowe at 31 December 1980. The two accounts with balances in them as at that date were debtors (debit balance £4,000) and provision for bad debts (credit balance £200). The debtors' account will be changing frequently during 1981. Whenever Rowe sells goods on credit he will debit this account and whenever the retailers pay him he will credit this account with the money received and any discount allowed. Also, at various dates during the year he may have to write off some of the debts as irrecoverable. This will require a credit entry in the debtors' account. The corresponding entry can now be made in the provision for bad debts account because it contains an amount earmarked specifically for this purpose.

Suppose that in 1981 Rowe wrote off £250 of debts as being irrecoverable. Before preparing the final accounts, the provision account will look like this:

Dr		Provision for bad debts account			Cr
1981		£	*1981*		£
1 Jan. – 31 Dec.	Sundry debtors	250	1 Jan. Balance b/d		200

Clearly the provision made at the end of 1980 is a slight under-estimate. All the £200 has been used and an extra £50 is needed to make up the deficiency. In addition it will be necessary to provide for the fact that some debtors at the end of 1981 will probably fail to pay.

Assume that Rowe's debtors are valued at £6,000 on 31 December 1981 and that he decides a 5% provision for likely bad debts is still about right. He will need a provision balance of £300 to meet this requirement. In order to achieve this he will need to make a credit entry for £350. This is made up of the £300 needed *plus* the £50 required to make up the deficiency from last year. After the final accounts have been prepared the situation will be as follows.

Dr		Provision for bad debts account			Cr
1981		£	*1981*		£
1 Jan. – 31 Dec.	Sundry debtors	250	1 Jan. Balance b/d		200
31 Dec.	Balance c/d	300	31 Dec. Profit and loss a/c		350
		550			550
			1982		
			1 Jan. Balance b/d		300

Profit and loss account for A. Rowe for the year ended 31 Dec. 1981

	£
Expenses	
Provision for bad debts	350

Balance sheet of A. Rowe as at 31 December 1981

		£
Current assets		
Debtors		6,000
less Provision for bad debts		300
		5,700

Note that the balance sheet entry consists of the two balances in the relevant accounts at 31 December. The profit and loss account entry is the amount needed to be withdrawn from profit in order to provide a balance of £300. This section is important so reread method 1 before attempting the following.

Self-check

Remind yourself of Simon Robinson's position at 31 December 1980 in the last self-check.

During 1981, his second year of trading, he had written off debts to the value of £110 and at the end of the year his debtors amounted to £1,500. He decided to retain a provision of 5% of outstanding debtors to allow for bad debts. Show his provision for bad debts account and relevant entries in the final accounts at the end of 1981.

ANSWER

Cr		Provision for bad debts account		Dr
1981		£	*1981*	£
1 Jan. – 31 Dec. Bad debts		110	1 Jan. Balance b/d	125
31 Dec. Balance c/d		75	31 Dec. Profit and loss a/c	60
		185		185
			1982	
			1 Jan. Balance b/d	75

Profit and loss account of Robinson, year ended 31 December 1981

	£
Expenses	
Provision for bad debts	60

Balance sheet of Robinson at 31 December 1981

		£
Current assets		
Debtors		1,500
less Provision for bad debts		75
		1,425

If you succeeded with this exercise you deserve a pat on the back. Provision for bad debts is usually regarded as the most difficult adjustment at this level. I will therefore explain again the process by which the above answer was achieved.

At the beginning of 1981 the credit balance of £125 in the provision account represented 5% of the debtors figure as at 31 December 1980. During 1981 bad debts actually written off against this provision amounted to £110, thus £15 of the provision was unused. At the end of 1981 you were told that the debtors amounted to £1,500 and that the provision was to be maintained at 5%. Thus the provision balance needed is £75, i.e. $^5/_{100} \times$ £1,500. As there is still a £15 balance within the provision account it requires only £60 from this year's profit to obtain the balance needed. Note that the balance sheet entry uses the two balances in the ledger accounts after the profit and loss account has been prepared, i.e. debtors' £1,500 and provision £75.

Method 2 This involves keeping separate accounts for bad debts and the provision. We will use the information relating to Rowe's accounts for 1981 so that we can compare the results with those obtained by using method 1.

Dr		Bad debts account		Cr
1981		£	*1981*	£
1 Jan. – 31 Dec.	Sundry debtors	250	31 Dec. Transferred to profit and loss account	250

Provision for bad debts account

1981	£	1981		£
Balance c/d	300	1 Jan.	Balance b/d	200
		31 Dec.	Profit and loss account	100
	300			300
		1982		
		1 Jan.	Balance b/d	300

Profit and loss account of A. Rowe, year ended 31 December 1981

	£
Expenses	
Bad debts	250
Provision for bad debts	100

Balance sheet of A. Rowe, as at 31 Dec. 1981

	£
Current assets	
Debtors	6,000
less Provision for bad debts	300
	5,700

Let's summarise what has happened.

- The actual bad debts for 1981 have been written off debtors as they occurred and then transferred to the profit and loss account at the end of the year.
- It is calculated that a provision balance of £300 is needed at the end of the year, i.e. $\frac{5}{100} \times £6,000$.
- The balance in the provision account will not have altered since last year. A credit entry for £100 is made to adjust this balance to the £300 needed and the double entry completed in the profit and loss account.
- The balance sheet contains the £6,000 balance for debtors and the £300 provision balance. As before the provision balance is deducted from outstanding debtors so that a true value can be placed on the asset, debtors.

In comparing this with method 1 you will notice that the real difference concerns the profit and loss account. Instead of one entry for £350 we now have two entries – £250 for actual bad debts and £100 adjustment to the provision. The net result is, of course, the same; i.e. £350 is being counted as the expense relating to bad debts. While the entry in the provision account at the end of the year differs, the final balance is exactly the same as with method 1. A final difference concerns the number of accounts used. Method 2 required an account for bad debts whereas in method 1 the bad debts were written off in the provision account and no bad debts account was needed.

Reread the explanation of method 2 before attempting the following.

║   *Self-check*

║   Rewrite the relevant accounts of Simon Robinson at the end of 1981 using method 2.

ANSWER

Dr			Bad debts account		Cr
1981		£	*1981*		£
1 Jan. – 31 Dec.	Sundry debtors	110	31 Dec.	Transferred to profit and loss account	110

	Provision for bad debts account				
1981		£	*1981*		£
31 Dec.	Profit and loss account	50	1 Jan.	Balance b/d	125
31 Dec.	Balance c/d	75			
		125			125
			1982		
			1 Jan.	Balance b/d	75

Profit and loss account of Robinson, year ended 31 December 1981

	£
Expenses	
Bad debts	110
less Provision for bad debts	(50)

Balance sheet of Robinson as at 31 December 1981

	£
Current assets	
Debtors	1,500
less Provision for bad debts	75
	1,425

The figure of £50 in the profit and loss account for the provision is placed in brackets to indicate that it is a deduction from the expenses. As you can see the two entries combined; i.e. the actual bad debts of £110 and the provision adjustment of minus £50 give the same final result as obtained by method 1 – a net £60 is being deducted from profits to cover bad debts. As an alternative to deducting the provision adjustment from expenses you could add the £50 back into the profits. In effect what has happened is that the amount of debtors is less than last year. To retain a 5% provision therefore needs *less* finance than we already have in the provision account. A debit entry in the provision account for £50 reduces the credit balance to the sum we require. Thus with this method you must be prepared to make adjustments on either side of the provision account as needed. A credit entry will increase the provision and a debit entry will reduce it.

Bad debts recovered

Sometimes businessmen receive a pleasant surprise in connection with bad debts. A debt that has been written off as irrecoverable is paid by the debtor. Suppose that on 7 May 1982 the wholesaler Rowe recovers a debt of £45 which he had written off in 1981. The cash book will be debited with the money received. The credit entry to be made varies according to which of the two methods of dealing with bad debts is used.

Method 1 The recovered debt will be credited to the provision for bad debts account where it will help to offset the bad debts written off in 1981.

Dr	Provision for bad debts		Cr
	1982		£
	1 Jan.	Balance b/d	300
	7 May	Cash book	45

Method 2 A separate account for bad debts recovered will be credited with the £45. This amount will be transferred to the profit and loss account at the end of the year along with any other recovered debts. For the sake of simplicity we will assume here that this was the only such recovery in 1982.

Dr		Bad debts recovered account		Cr
1982		£	*1982*	£
31 Dec.	Transferred to profit and loss account	45	7 May Cash book	45
		—		—

Profit and loss account, year ended 31 December 1982

	£
Expenses	
less Bad debt recovered	(45)

The £45 is shown in brackets to indicate that it will be deducted from the expenses for 1982. Alternatively, the sum could be added to the gross profit and other incomes such as rent received.

Whichever method is being followed this transaction is of such an unusual nature that it would probably be journalised.

Self-check

During 1982, Simon Robinson's third year of trading, he wrote off debts to the value of £130 and on 8 June recovered one debt of £30 which he had written off in 1981. At the end of 1982 his debtors amounted to £1,600 and he decided to retain a provision of 5% of outstanding debtors to allow for bad debts. Show his accounts as they would appear using method 1 and method 2.

ANSWER

Method 1

Dr			Provision for bad debts account			Cr
1982			£	*1982*		£
1 Jan. – 31 Dec.	Bad debts	130		1 Jan.	Balance b/d	75
31 Dec.	Balance c/d	80		8 June	Cash book	30
				31 Dec.	Profit and loss account	105
		210				210
				1983		
				1 Jan.	Balance b/d	80

Profit and loss account of Robinson, year ended 31 December 1982

	£
Expenses	
Provision for bad debts	105

Balance sheet of Robinson as at 31 Dec. 1982

	£
Current assets	
Debtors	1,600
less Provision for bad debts	80
	1,520

Method 2

Dr			Bad debts account		Cr
1982		£	*1982*		£
1 Jan. – 31 Dec.	Sundry debtors	130	31 Dec.	Transferred to profit and loss account	130

Dr			Bad debts recovered account		Cr
1982		£	*1982*		£
31 Dec.	Transferred to profit and loss account	30	8 June	Cash book	30

Dr	Provision for bad debts account				Cr
1982		£	*1982*		£
31 Dec.	Balance c/d	80	1 Jan.	Balance b/d	75
			31 Dec.	Profit and loss account	5
		80			80
			1983		
			1 Jan.	Balance b/d	80

Profit and loss account of Robinson, year ended 31 Dec. 1982

	£
Expenses	
Bad debts	130
Bad debts recovered	(30)
Provision for bad debts	5

Balance sheet of Robinson as at 31 Dec. 1982

	£
Current assets	
Debtors	1,600
less Provision for bad debts	80
	1,520

As you can see the balance sheet entry is identical whichever
method is used. The entries in the profit and loss account do
differ in form but the effect is the same, i.e. a 'net' effect of
reducing profits by £105 in 1982. You can decide for yourself
which method you prefer. Personally, I prefer the logic and
greater simplicity of method 1. In examinations, however, you
may not be given a choice. The way the question is worded may
indicate that you have to follow one particular method.

The following question will help to test your understanding of
this chapter and provide additional practice in preparing final
accounts.

Review

Trial balance of A. Rowe as at 31 December 1983

	£ dr	£ cr
Capital (1 Jan.)		86,000
Stocks (1 Jan.)	60,000	
Leasehold premises	120,000	
Fixtures and fittings	10,000	
Motor vehicles	30,000	
Debtors	15,000	
Creditors		40,000
Advertising and insurance	2,000	
Salaries and wages	45,000	
Provision for bad debts (1 Jan.)		500
Rates	1,000	
Discount received		1,000
Discount allowed	2,000	
Purchases	80,000	
Sales		150,000
Heating and lighting	2,000	
Bank	8,500	
Sundry expenses	2,000	
Mortgage on premises		100,000
	377,500	377,500

Taking into account the following matters, prepare a trading and profit and loss account for the year ended 31 December 1981 and a balance sheet at that date.

a On 31 December, Rowe reviews his debtors and decides that £1,000 of the £15,000 due should be written off as bad debts. The provision is to remain at 5% of the outstanding debtors after bad debts have been written off.

b A bill for £500 electricity is outstanding on 31 December.

c Insurance prepaid on 31 December amounts to £200.

d Stocks at 31 December were valued at £70,000.

ANSWER

Trading and profit and loss account of A. Rowe for the year ended 31 December 1983

	£	£
Sales		150,000
less *Cost of goods sold*		
Opening stocks	60,000	
add Purchases	80,000	
	140,000	
less Closing stocks	70,000	
		70,000
Gross profit		80,000
Discount received		1,000
		81,000
less *Expenses*		
Salaries and wages	45,000	
Provision for bad debts	1,200	
Heating and lighting	2,500	
Advertising and insurance	1,800	
Rates	1,000	
Discount allowed	2,000	
Sundry expenses	2,000	
		55,500
Net profit		25,500

Balance sheet of A. Rowe as at 31 December 1983

	£	£		£	£
Capital	86,000		*Fixed assets*		
add Net profit	25,500		Premises	120,000	
		111,500	Fixtures and fittings	10,000	
			Motor vehicles	30,000	
					160,000
			Current assets		
Long-term liabilities			Stock	70,000	
Mortgage		100,000	Debtors 14,000		
			less		
			Provision 700	13,300	
Current liabilities			Bank	8,500	
Creditors	40,000		Insurance		
Accrual – electricity	500		prepaid	200	92,000
		40,500			
		252,000			252,000

As the provision for bad debts is the only really new element in the above review, I will explain how the profit and loss account and balance sheet entries were derived. I have used the first method you were shown. The actual bad debts of £1,000 left the provision of £500 deficient by £500. As a provision of £700 is needed at the end of the year (5% of £14,000 – outstanding debtors), £1,200 must come from this year's profits – £500 to make up the deficiency and £700 to establish the new provision. The account will look like this:

Dr			Provision for bad debts account		Cr
1983		£	*1983*		£
31 Dec.	Sundry debtors	1,000	1 Jan.	Balance b/d	500
31 Dec.	Balance c/d	700	31 Dec.	Profit and loss account	1,200
		1,700			1,700
			1984		
			1 Jan.	Balance b/d	700

When you are asked to prepare final accounts from a trial balance with adjustments it is not essential to do the individual ledger accounts. You can obtain the correct answer arithmetically, e.g.

	£
Opening provision	500
less Bad debts	1,000
Provision remaining (or deficit)	(500)
Provision needed	700
Therefore required from profit	1,200

If you used the second method of dealing with bad debts you would have ended up with two entries in the profit and loss account:

- £1,000 actual bad debts;
- £200 provision adjustment (to raise £500 to £700).

The balance sheet entry would have been the same.

14 | Estimating and recording depreciation

In this chapter we are going to look at the way in which capital expenditure on a fixed asset can be spread over the life of the asset. This is done so that a fair amount of the expense can be recorded each year in the profit and loss account and a truer, more up-to-date valuation of the asset can be shown in the balance sheet. Two methods of book-keeping will be considered because both are encountered in examination questions. Before you begin this chapter you are advised to reread the section on depreciation in Chapter 5 and on capital expenditure in Chapter 10.

Estimating depreciation

Most fixed assets have a limited number of years of useful life. Depreciation is the name given to the process by which these assets decrease in value over their lifetime. The only way to be absolutely sure of the amount of depreciation that has taken place is to sell the asset. Thus if a motor vehicle cost £4,000 on 1 January 1980 and was sold for £3,000 on 31 December 1980 we can quite safely say that depreciation on that asset for the year 1980 amounted to £1,000.

People in business are not, however, in it to sell their fixed assets. To do so simply to know precisely how much depreciation has occurred is clearly out of the question. Therefore some means of estimating the amount of the depreciation is needed. The most accurate way would be to obtain a valuation, by someone qualified, of what each asset is worth at the end of every year of trading. Thus machinery valued at £1,800 at 31 December 1980 might be revalued at £1,600 on 31 December 1981. We could therefore state that £200 would be a reliable estimate of the depreciation on machinery for the year ended 31 December

1981. In a small business with few fixed assets revaluing the fixed assets each year might not be too difficult. The problems arise when you attempt to do this in larger businesses which possess a greater number and variety of fixed assets. Accountants attempt to overcome these problems by using one of the following methods to estimate depreciation.

Equal instalment method

As its name suggests, this involves depreciating an asset by an equal amount throughout its useful life. For example, equipment purchased for £10,000 on 1 January 1980 might be expected to last for ten years. To depreciate this in equal instalments would require an amount of £1,000 to be written off the value of the asset each year. A simple formula can be applied to obtain the annual amount of depreciation:

$$\frac{\text{cost of asset}}{\text{estimated life in years}} = \frac{£10,000}{10} = £1,000 \text{ depreciation per annum.}$$

Many fixed assets will have some value even when their working life is over. This is known as their scrap value. The above formula can be adapted to allow for an asset having some value as scrap:

$$\frac{\text{cost of asset less estimated scrap value}}{\text{estimated life in years}}$$

Suppose that the equipment in the above example had an estimated scrap value of £500. The amount of depreciation to be written off each year for the next ten years would be:

$$\frac{£10,000 \text{ less } £500}{10 \text{ years}} = \frac{£9,500}{10} = £950 \text{ per annum.}$$

Self-check

A new company began trading on 1 January 1981. Its fixed assets included new machinery which it had purchased for £13,000. This machinery had a life expectancy of eight years with an estimated scrap value of £1,000 after that time.

1 Calculate the amount of depreciation to be written off
   each year.
2 State the value of this machinery at the end of 1984.

ANSWERS

1 $\dfrac{\text{£13,000 less £1,000}}{8 \text{ years}} = \dfrac{\text{£12,000}}{8} = \text{£1,500 per annum.}$

2 Cost less accumulated depreciation to date = current value of
  asset, i.e. £13,000 less £6,000 = £7,000. Four years' depreciation will have been written off this asset by the end of 1984.
  Thus at £1,500 per annum a total of £6,000 will have been
  written off, leaving the machinery valued at £7,000.

It is possible to obtain a valuation of an asset at any stage of its
working life by referring to a schedule such as the one below.
This relates to the machinery in our last self-check.

Machinery X: cost £13,000

Year	Depn for the year ended 31 Dec.	Accumulated depn up to the year ended 31 Dec.	Asset value at 31 Dec.
	£	£	£
1981	1,500	1,500	11,500
1982	1,500	3,000	10,000
1983	1,500	4,500	8,500
1984	1,500	6,000	7,000
1985	1,500	7,500	5,500

Each year the same amount of depreciation is being written off
the asset's value. The column for accumulated depreciation
enables us to see at a glance the total amount of depreciation that
has been written off to date. Deducting this figure from the cost
of the machinery provides us with its value at the end of any year
in the schedule. Thus by the end of December 1985 five years'
depreciation, i.e. £7,500, will have been written off and the
machinery will be worth £5,500.

This method is also known as straight-line depreciation
because the amount is the same each year.

Reducing instalment method

This involves depreciating the asset by a fixed percentage each year based on the value of the asset at the beginning of that year.

Suppose, for example, that the company which purchased the machinery for £13,000 on 1 January 1981 decided to depreciate at 10% per annum by this method. At the end of 1981 which is its first year of trading, the depreciation to be written off will be

$$\frac{10}{100} \times £13,000 = £1,300.$$

At the beginning of 1982 the machinery will be valued at £11,700, i.e. its cost less depreciation to date, or £13,000 less £1,300. The rate of depreciation remains at 10% but the actual amount of depreciation to be written off for 1982 will be

$$\frac{10}{100} \times £11,700 = £1,170.$$

You can now see why this method is known as the reducing instalment method. Although the rate of depreciation stays the same it is being calculated on the diminishing asset value. Thus each year the actual amount of depreciation written off will be less.

Self-check

Complete the following depreciation schedule for machinery X, using the reducing instalment method with a fixed rate of 10%. Depreciation should be calculated to the nearest £1.

Machinery X: cost £13,000

Year	Depn for the year ended 31 Dec.	Accumulated depn up to the year ended 31 Dec.	Asset value at 31 Dec.
	£	£	£
1981	1,300	1,300	11,700
1982	1,170	2,470	
1983			9,477
1984			
1985			

ANSWER

	£	£	£
1981	1,300	1,300	11,700
1982	1,170	2,470	10,530
1983	1,053	3,523	9,477
1984	948	4,471	8,529
1985	853	5,324	7,676

Since depreciation is very much an estimate, there is no point in calculating it in pence. The nearest £1 will always suffice when using this method.

Recording depreciation

We can now turn to recording depreciation in the ledger. There are two main methods used. One I shall call the simple method and the other the accumulated depreciation method.

Depreciation – the simple method

This is the method introduced in Chapter 5. Each asset which is to be depreciated has its own depreciation account. At the end of each financial year the asset account is credited with the amount of depreciation for that year and the depreciation account is debited. The entry in depreciation account is then transferred to the profit and loss account as the expense for the period. Finally the asset account is balanced and the balance sheet shows the final value of the asset by deducting the year's depreciation from the asset's value at the start of the year.

An example will help to make this clear. We will use the information provided by the depreciation schedule in the last self-check showing the accounts completed for the first two years. Trace the double entries as they occur in the ledger accounts and then look at the entries in the final accounts.

Dr			Machinery account		Cr
1981		£	*1981*		£
1 Jan.	Bank	13,000	31 Dec.	Depreciation	1,300
			31 Dec.	Balance c/d	11,700
		13,000			13,000
1982			*1982*		
1 Jan.	Balance b/d	11,700	31 Dec.	Depreciation	1,170
			31 Dec.	Balance c/d	10,530
		11,700			11,700
1983					
1 Jan.	Balance b/d	10,530			

		Depreciation on machinery account		
1981		£	*1981*	£
			31 Dec. Transferred to profit	
31 Dec.	Machinery	1,300	and loss account	1,300
1982			*1982*	
			Transferred to profit	
31 Dec.	Machinery	1,170	1 Jan. and loss account	1,170

Profit and loss account, year ended 31 December 1981

£

Expenses
Depreciation on machinery 1,300

Balance sheet, as at 31 December 1981

	£	£
Fixed assets		
Machinery	13,000	
less Depn for year	1,300	
		11,700

Profit and loss account, year ended 31 December 1982

£

Expenses
Depreciation on machinery 1,170

Balance sheet as at 31 December 1982

	£	£
Fixed assets		
Machinery	11,700	
less Depn for year	1,170	
		10,530

Self-check

Complete the accounts relating to the machinery and its depreciation up to the end of December 1983.

ANSWER

Dr			Machinery account			Cr
1983		£	*1983*			£
1 Jan.	Balance b/d	10,530	31 Dec.	Depreciation		1,053
			31 Dec.	Balance c/d		9,477
		10,530				10,530
1984						
1 Jan.	Balance b/d	9,477				

		Depreciation on machinery account			
1983		£	*1983*		£
			31 Dec.	Transferred to profit	
31 Dec.	Machinery	1,053		and loss account	1,053

Profit and loss account, year ended 31 December 1983

	£
Expenses	
Depn on machinery	1,053

Balance sheet as at 31 December 1983

	£	£
Fixed assets		
Machinery	10,530	
less Depn for year	1,053	
		9,477

Depreciation – the accumulation method

Compared with the method just discussed this method requires one additional account which is used to maintain a record of the depreciation accumulated to date. This account is usually called the provision for depreciation account though a more accurate title would be accumulated depreciation account.

This method involves a debit entry each year in the depreciation account for that year's depreciation. Instead of making the credit entry in the asset account, however, it is made in the provision for depreciation account. Using the example of the machinery being depreciated by reducing instalments the ledger accounts for the first two years will look like this:

Dr			Machinery account			Cr
1981		£	*1981*			£
1 Jan.	Bank	13,000	31 Dec.	Balance c/d		13,000
		——				——
1982			*1982*			
1 Jan.	Balance b/d	13,000	31 Dec.	Balance c/d		13,000
		——				——
1983						
1 Jan.	Balance b/d	13,000				

Dr		Provision for depreciation on machinery account			Cr
1981		£	*1981*		£
31 Dec.	Balance c/d	1,300	31 Dec.	Depreciation	1,300
		——			——
1982			*1982*		
31 Dec.	Balance c/d	2,470	1 Jan.	Balance b/d	1,300
			31 Dec.	Depreciation	1,170
		——			——
		2,470			2,470
		——			——
			1983		
			1 Jan.	Balance b/d	2,470

Depreciation on machinery account

1981		£	1981		£
31 Dec.	Provision for depn	1,300	31 Dec.	Transferred to profit and loss account	1,300
1982			1982		
31 Dec.	Provision for depn	1,170	31 Dec.	Transferred to profit and loss account	1,170

As you can see, the depreciation account is substantially the same as in the simpler method – only the description has changed slightly. The real difference lies with the asset account. This now shows the value of the asset at cost with no depreciation being deducted from it within the account. You might argue, with good reason, that it is not worth balancing this account each year. It is, however, probably a good thing to continue to do so as it does indicate that the account has been looked at each year. To obtain the value of the asset at any date it is now necessary to combine the asset balance with the accumulated depreciation balance in the provision account. Thus the value of the machinery at 31 December 1982 will be £10,530, i.e.

		£	
Cost		13,000	(from the asset account)
less Depn to date		2,470	(from the provision account)
		10,530	

The profit and loss account entries will be exactly the same as they were when using the other method. The balance sheet entries will differ, however, because we will always be showing the value of the asset at cost less the accumulated depreciation to date. This difference will not be apparent in the first year because the accumulated depreciation is identical to the first year's depreciation. From the second year, however, you will notice the difference. It should be emphasised that the actual final value of the asset shown in the balance sheet will be the same which-ever method is used. Prove this to yourself by comparing the two entries below with those on pages 212–13.

Balance sheet as at 31 December 1981

	£	£
Fixed assets		
Machinery at cost	13,000	
less Depn to date	1,300	
		11,700

Balance sheet as at 31 December 1982

	£
Fixed assets	
Machinery at cost	13,000
less Depn to date	2,470
	10,530

Self-check

Complete the accounts relating to the machinery and its depreciation up to the end of December 1983. This time, use the provision for depreciation method.

ANSWER

Dr			Machinery account		Cr
1983		£	*1983*		£
1 Jan.	Balance b/d	13,000	31 Dec.	Balance c/d	13,000
1984					
1 Jan.	Balance b/d	13,000			

		Provision for depreciation on machinery account			
1983		£	*1983*		£
31 Dec.	Balance c/d	3,523	1 Jan.	Balance b/d	2,470
			31 Dec.	Depreciation	1,053
		3,523			3,523
			1984		
			1 Jan.	Balance b/d	3,523

Depreciation on machinery account

1983		£	1983		£
31 Dec.	Provision for depn	1,053	31 Dec.	Transferred to profit and loss account	1,053

Profit and loss account, year ended 31 December 1983

£

Expenses
Depn on machinery   1,053

Balance sheet as at 31 December 1983

	£	£
Fixed assets		
Machinery at cost	13,000	
less Depreciation to date	3,523	
		9,477

Compare this solution with the one on page 213 and you will see that the net result is exactly the same. You might wonder, therefore, why the second method is needed. This query is answered in *Practical Accounts 2,* where you are introduced to the accounts of limited companies.

One aspect of the second method of accounting for depreciation that often causes problems to students involves the name of the ledger account in which the aggregate depreciation is accumulated. The title 'provision for depreciation account' gives an impression that finance has actually been set aside which can be used to purchase a replacement for the fixed asset when its working life is over. This is a false impression. The provision for depreciation account is simply an account in which the aggregate or total depreciation written off an asset is accumulated each year. For this reason, the term 'accumulated' or 'aggregate depreciation account' would be a more accurate title. There is, of course, nothing to prevent a businessman from keeping back a greater amount of the net profit for use within the business to replace worn-out assets. This, however, is not automatic on creating a provision for depreciation account – a conscious policy decision would have to be made to retain or 'plough back' profits for this use.

Further calculations

Until now we have been concerned only with calculations of depreciation on fixed assets which have been in the business for a complete financial year. In practice there will be occasions when assets are bought part-way through the business's financial year. When this happens you would be expected to calculate the correct proportion of depreciation relating to that year for inclusion in the accounts.

For example the business whose accounts we have been showing in this chapter has a financial year which ends at 31 December. Suppose that it purchases equipment for £6,000 on 1 July 1982 and estimates that it will last for ten years and have a scrap value of £200 at the end of that time. Depreciation using the equal instalment method will be:

$$\frac{\text{cost of asset less estimated scrap value}}{\text{estimated life in years}} = \frac{£6,000 - £200}{10 \text{ years}} = \frac{£5,800}{10}$$

= £580 depreciation per annum.

In 1982, however, it would be wrong to depreciate the equipment by £580 because the asset has been in use for only six months. The correct amount of depreciation for 1982 is thus

$6/12$ or $1/2 \times £580 = £290$.

> ### *Self-check*
>
> The same business bought a motor vehicle for £5,000 on 1 April 1982. It was decided to depreciate it by 30% per annum using the reducing instalment method. Calculate the amount of depreciation to be written off in the financial year ended 31 December 1982.

ANSWER

$$\frac{30}{100} \times \frac{£5,000}{1} \times \frac{3}{4} = £1,125.$$

30% of £5,000 would give the amount of depreciation to be written off in 1982 if the asset had been used for a full year. As it was used for only nine months in 1982 the proportionate amount of depreciation to be written off is

$9/12$ or $3/4$.

Take care when calculating these proportions. In most examination questions the asset is purchased at the beginning or the end of a month. While 1 April to 31 December will be counted as nine months, if the asset had been purchased on 30 April it will have been used for only eight months in 1982. Thus in the latter case the proportion would be

$^8/_{12}$ or $^2/_3$.

You might wonder how you would deal with the depreciation on an asset purchased on, say, 19 September. Should the proportion be calculated on the number of days the asset has been used during the year? The answer to this is 'no'. Depreciation is only an estimate. It is quite sufficient, therefore, to calculate it solely on the total number of complete months in which it is used in that first year. Thus in this case the proportionate amount of depreciation would be

$^3/_{12}$ or $^1/_4$

because the asset was in use for only the three whole months of October, November and December.

Disposal of assets and adjustments to depreciation

When a fixed asset is sold it is very unlikely that it will realise a figure exactly equal to its value in the accounts. For this to happen the depreciation estimate would have had to have been 100% accurate!

If the asset sells for less than its book value we might say that we have made a loss on sale whereas in fact we have probably underestimated the amount of depreciation to be written off the value of the asset. If the asset sells for more than its book value we might say that we have made a profit on sale. Probably the truth is that we have overestimated the amount of depreciation to be written off. When either of these eventualities occurs, an adjustment must be made to the depreciation shown in the profit and loss account for the year in which the asset is sold.

For example, a motor vehicle which has a book value of £2,000 is sold for £1,800. The £200 loss on sale or under provision of depreciation will be added to the expenses thus:

Profit and loss account

£

Expenses

Under provision of depn
 on motor vehicle   200

If the vehicle has been sold for £2,300 when valued in the books at £2,000 the profit on sale or overprovision of depreciation could be shown thus:

Profit and loss account

£

Expenses

Over provision of depn
 on motor vehicle   (300)

The brackets around the £300 indicate that this amount is deducted from the other expenses for the year.

Review

If you have understood this chapter you should be able to answer the following question. It also tests a number of other accounting aspects dealt with earlier.

Examine the following trial balance of M. Trigg, retailer, taken from his books at 30 June 1982.

	£ dr	£ cr
Fixed assets (at cost)	40,000	
Provision for depn on fixed assets		4,000
Stock	8,000	
Debtors	1,500	
Provision for bad debts		100
Bank		100
Creditors		500
Cash	200	
Capital		26,000
Sales		90,000
Purchases	60,000	
Wages	4,000	
Drawings	1,000	
General expenses	6,000	
	120,700	120,700

Prepare a trading and profit and loss account for the year ended 30 June 1982 and a balance sheet at that date, taking into consideration the following:

a Stock at 30 June 1982, £10,000.
b Fixed assets are to be depreciated by 10% on cost.
c Bad debts of £80 are to be written off and the provision adjusted to 5% of outstanding debtors.
d General expenses include a prepayment of £200 rent for July 1982.

ANSWER

Trading and profit and loss account of M. Trigg for the year ended 30 June 1982

	£	£
Sales		90,000
less *Cost of sales*		
Opening stock	8,000	
add Purchases	60,000	
	68,000	
less Closing stock	10,000	
		58,000
Gross profit		32,000
Expenses		
Wages	4,000	
Depn on fixed assets	4,000	
Provision for bad debts	51	
General expenses	5,800	
		13,851
Net profit		18,149

Balance sheet of M. Trigg as at 30 June 1982

	£	£		£	£	£
Capital	26,000		Fixed assets at cost	40,000		
add Profit	18,149		less Aggregate depn	8,000		
	44,149					32,000
less Drawings	1,000		Current assets			
		43,149	Stock		10,000	
			Debtors	1,420		
Current liabilities			less Provision for			
Creditors	500		bad debts	71		
Bank overdraft	100	600			1,349	
			Cash		200	
			Prepaid rent		200	
						11,749
		43,749				43,749

Postscript

Having worked your way through this book, you are now ready to further your knowledge of accounting. You will find *Practical Accounts 2* by George Bright an ideal way of continuing your studies.

Index